AMBITION

Also by Ellie Rubin

Bulldog: Spirit of the New Entrepreneur

AMBITION
7 RULES FOR GETTING THERE

ELLIE RUBIN

Copyright © 2004 by Ellie Rubin

All rights reserved. No part of this publication may be reproduced or transmitted in any form or by any means, electronic or mechanical, including photocopying, recording, or any information storage and retrieval system, without permission in writing from the publisher.

Published in 2008 by
BPS Books
Toronto, Canada
www.bpsbooks.net
A division of
Bastian Publishing Services Ltd.

First published in 2004 by Penguin Group (Canada)

Author representation: Westwood Creative Artists
94 Harbord Street, Toronto, Ontario M5S 1G6

ISBN 978-0-9809231-1-7

Cataloguing in Publication Data available from Library and Archives Canada.

Cover Design: Greg Devitt Design

*For Chloë Lane and Alexandra Jade
In memory of Alex J. Rubin*

At the age of six I wanted to be a cook.
At seven I wanted to be Napoleon.
And my ambition has been growing steadily ever since.
—*Salvador Dali*

CONTENTS

Introduction: A Winning Ambitionist Approach		xi
RULE 1	DISCOVERY	1
RULE 2	FOCUS	25
RULE 3	BELONGING	47
RULE 4	MOMENTUM	83
RULE 5	BALANCE	113
RULE 6	MATURITY	139
RULE 7	BELIEF	159
Epilogue: Getting There		189
Notes		193
Acknowledgments		197
Making Contact		201
Index		203

INTRODUCTION
A Winning Ambitionist Approach

I am neither an optimist nor pessimist, but a possibilist.
—Max Lerner

It haunts us. It guides us. It torments us. It motivates us. It is called ambition. And however it moves you, it's a loaded word. As an entrepreneur, I always took the concept of ambition for granted; it was, after all, at the heart of all that I did. But it wasn't until a few years ago that I decided to revisit this word and all its connotations.

Ken Whyte, former editor in chief of the *National Post*, had invited me for lunch to discuss the possibility of writing a weekly column for the newspaper. Based on the success of my first bestseller, *Bulldog: Spirit of the New Entrepreneur*, and the work I was doing in the area of self-motivation and career development, the column would highlight the questions relating to work, success, and achievement that over the years I had collected from my readers and speaking audiences. We agreed that in addressing these questions every week, I would focus on insights, tips, tactics, and strategies for all kinds of work, entrepreneurial and otherwise.

With the topics in hand for the new column, we had just one more major element to cover—what to call it? As Ken and I chatted about work issues, what matters to people, success, and the barriers to obtaining goals, he said, "Why don't we simply call the column Ambition, since that's what all of this is really about?" It was perfect, and at that moment I knew that I would not only commit to writing a weekly column exploring this basic human impulse, but that perhaps it would be the jumping-off point for another book. And it was.

Over the past few years, the more I looked into the notion of ambition and how it relates to clients, readers, associates, friends, and community, the more I began to recognize patterns in both human reaction to and understanding of this word. Here are a few of the key observations that surfaced.

Whether it was a high-powered financier, a university student with a plan, or an entrepreneur with a list of successes attached to her name, whenever I asked people what comes to mind when they think of the word *ambition* I'd be met with a reflective pause. What would follow was a response that, in one form or another, would almost invariably attest to an ongoing struggle to reconcile two opposing forces. "Ambition for me is about following my dreams without leaving my loved ones behind" was one variant. "Ambition is about struggling to have it all while knowing I never will" was another. What came through, in other words, was an everlasting conflict between what people desired (fame, money, power, freedom) and what they felt they were able to sacrifice (time, family, freedom) to get it.

Complicating the picture is the fact that ambition continues to suffer a longstanding, old-world, negative reputation. It brings up images of the wealthy risk taker and the mover and shaker, the political wheeler and dealer, and the one who's willing to do whatever it takes to get ahead, even if it means sacrificing friends, family, and colleagues. Today, for many, ambition is synonymous with mistrust, closely aligned with such international corporate leaders as those at Enron, who mismanaged their ambition and destroyed their credibility with the general public and shareholders alike.

And yet at the same time, among those I interviewed I detected a desire, even a need, to redefine ambition in a more positive, new-world light as a means of resolving their ambivalence about attaining success at the cost of tampering with their values. That need has only been heightened since 9/11 and the ongoing terrorism campaigns that feature in the headlines every day, along with rising unemployment figures, corporate scandals, and stock market fluctuations. With these as a backdrop to everyday living, along with a greater need for security and success, many of us have chosen to pause, gain new perspective, and question our values and what we really want out of life.

"People are looking to have careers that allow more balance in terms of their family life, leisure, and avocational interests," says Barbara Laporte, a lifework consultant for the Career and Lifework Center at the University of Minnesota. "Their goals now aren't so much about just career planning, but life planning." And with good reason. A 1998 Statistics Canada General Social Survey on time use found that one-third of Canadians aged twenty-five to forty-four identified themselves as workaholics, and that more than half admitted to worrying that they don't have enough time to spend with their family and friends. More generally, the survey results indicated that more than one in four Canadians over the age of fifteen described themselves as workaholics. In *Driven to Excel: A Portrait of Canada's Workaholics,* Anna Kemeny notes that "this proportion agrees with studies done in the United States which estimate that approximately 27% to 30% of the U.S. population is 'addicted' to work." In the US, 78 percent of those questioned in an *American Demographics* survey said that since September 11, their families have become more of a priority. And similar statistics concerning the conflict between personal values and vocational demands are reflected in most Western societies worldwide. In short, the times demand a reassessment of ambition and a more holistic approach to its definition.

Yet, people are still tantalized by ambition. Their desire to achieve success and advance their careers seems to have grown, especially if the number of books dedicated to these topics is any indication. What people crave, then, is a seamless combination of motivation, inspiration, and practical tactics that will allow them to determine the best means to manage their ambition according to their own personal success meter and their own personal values. In my experience, people are also looking for a set of guiding principles that will encourage them to improvise and experiment with their understanding of ambition.

When I first contemplated writing a book about ambition, my questions were wide and deep: Does ambition evolve over time? Are there distinct phases? What is ambition made of? Is there a literature around ambition? Is there a key parable or fable about it? Does it have limits or boundaries? Is it a fatal flaw, a sin? What are its more positive qualities? What is its aim—success, achievement, power, money, control, self-definition? Are there separate male and female ambitions? What are the differences and similarities? Does ambition have a pace or speed? Is it always associated with movement, energy, and activity?

My line of thinking soon changed, however. As I conducted research in the field with clients, polled audiences I presented to, and interviewed talented individuals I had the pleasure of meeting, I realized that the meaning of ambition didn't reside in the "big" questions. Rather, as people told me their stories, distinct themes emerged that cut across industry, level of success, and ambitious tendencies. I found that by organizing these ideas into a set of attainable rules, I could provide a way of clarifying the meaning, relevance, and value of an individual's ambitious journey in the here and now.

The more I ventured forward with this notion of a set of rules, the more I found that people are frightened by raw ambition. They're searching for a way to design their ambition so that they can live with today's familiar dichotomies: between what they want and what their strengths are; between what they started out believing in and what experience has taught them to value; and between who they're spending time with and what they really want to think and dream about. Ultimately, if people can find a way to define ambition according to a set of rules that are cyclical, then regardless of where they find themselves in their own life journey, they can tap into this process and easily apply it again and again, each time defining "getting there" differently.

In *Bulldog*, I coined the phrase "I entrepreneur" as a means of encouraging readers to think and act like an entrepreneur, whether they ever started a company or not. In this book, I introduce the notion of the "ambitionist" as someone who chooses to design ambition to suit his or her vocational and personal needs and desires. By providing this twenty-first-century notion of ambition as a positive catalyst for change, career shaping, team building, and personal and vocational growth, I hope to give you, the reader, a new vision of the ambitious journey.

The seven rules for ambition that evolved carefully build upon each other and may be cycled through once or many times during a lifetime. They include the excitement of discovery, the power to make responsible choices, the momentum gained through teamwork, the art of balance, and the ability to view failure as a valuable opportunity for learning. They also include the freedom that comes with redefining personal values and the deep satisfactions of altruism.

I present this book as one answer to the search for values and survival strategies in today's world. My hope is that by incorporating these seven essential rules for the ambitionist, and their attendant strategies, you will learn how to successfully redesign your ambition—as a means of not only achieving your career goals but also gaining a better sense of well-being and life satisfaction.

As the structure of the book emerged through ongoing research and feedback, the question became, Who to interview to bring these seven rules to life, to illustrate their importance and relevance? The obvious answer was to collect stories and experiences from a host of highly successful businesspeople as a means of inspiring readers and making the points stick. But being an eclectic individual, I found myself drawn to the idea of approaching high-profile people in a whole range of fields. I would look for those who had not only attained a certain level of success but who managed their ambitions while pursuing them wholeheartedly.

And so my search for fascinating and inspiring stories began. And I have found them—from the diverse worlds of theater, environmental policy, and medical science to those of clairvoyance, extreme sports, and culinary arts. I am indebted to each and every one of these people for their honesty, insight, and willingness to explore ambition in all its many facets. And in the process of hearing their stories, my own sense of ambition and how I plan to redesign it in my own life work was reignited.

As I wrote this book I kept asking myself, Is it a guide, a set of rules to live by, or a collection of inspiring stories? Is it the beginning of an exploration or the means to an end? Because these seven rules also reflect the seven stages in the cycle of ambition, each of you will read this book in a different light by virtue of where you are in your own ambitious journey. My hope is that you will find each of the seven rules a starting point to determine where you're at in relation to ambition, and take away a few immediate tactics that you can apply to your world as you struggle to wrap your arms around this ever-present topic. Some stories will sing to you, others will entertain you. Some ideas, no doubt, will seem far-fetched and others will hit a nerve that will force you to re-examine and regroup. My own continuing struggle with ambition was sometimes illuminated, often thrown into upheaval, and mostly up for reinterpretation.

But I also came out the other end of this process recognizing that everyone has ambition. It's not just reserved for the wealthy, the powerful, and the driven. It includes people who are trying to decide on a career path, or who have been in a particular career for many years but are looking for new horizons, or who feel out of place in their current job and are looking to make the transition into another one. And so, regardless of whether your ambition is great or modest, I believe that these seven rules will enable you to design your ambitious journey. They'll help you identify what you do best, how to make the decisions that will get you there, who will be your mentors and team along the way, how to bounce back from failure, and what values you want to bring with you. To be an ambitionist is really about defining success on your own terms. It's a testament to individuality—and ultimately a celebration of the possibilities in whatever journey you've chosen.

RULE 1
DISCOVERY

> In the depths of winter I finally learned
> there was in me an invincible summer.
> —*Albert Camus*

"It always began with a stroll. And as I walked or sauntered or ambled along, I would discover or rediscover what it was that I was good at . . . and what I was going to do about it." This is how my interview with Anthony E. Zuiker begins. Over many cups of coffee, I learned how a tram operator on the graveyard shift in Las Vegas became the creator and executive producer for television's *CSI* (Crime Scene Investigation), the highest-rated show on television. His story is one about discovery, and that's the starting point for any ambitionist.

Anthony first realized what he was good at in grade ten when he chose public speaking as an elective. Despite some initial stumbles, by the end of the year he broke into the county finals and landed second place. Walking home from that competition, he had his first discovery: he could write and he could get up on stage. *And* he liked it. Little did he know how important his public speaking ability would be in the career he eventually created for himself.

Several years later, with two college degrees in his pocket, Anthony expected to land a plum job that would test his writing abilities. But things didn't work out that way. He first got a stint at Dean Witter as a wire operator, and then took a sales job for Merrill Lynch. These jobs neither motivated him nor called upon his writing and speaking skills in the way he imagined, and the initial lure of making money waned with each passing day. What did not wane, however, was his love of writing and his enjoyment in entertaining people. "So on the side, I wrote letters, press releases, any kind of copy for executives who had no talent, and charged them three hundred bucks a pop."

At twenty-six, Anthony was still looking for a place to showcase his writing talents. When the Mirage Hotel opened its doors in Las Vegas, he applied and took the only job he could get: tram operator on the graveyard shift for eight dollars an hour. A far cry from the writer/entertainer image he had of himself, but he hoped to work his way up the hotel ladder and land a position in the advertising department. "While I rode the tram throughout the night, I had to converse with tourists from every country. To make my job more fun, I memorized how to say things in a variety of languages: 'How are you today? Can I help you with that?' I ended up creating tourist pamphlets in several languages. Before I knew it, all the bellmen, the managers, and the front-desk clerks were asking me for these booklets to help them serve their foreign clients. I did it on my own penny and it was fun. But it certainly wasn't paying the rent."

It did give him visibility, though, and sure enough, he got a job in the advertising department. But his assignments were limited, and once again Anthony wondered if and when he'd find a way to test what he thought were his true talents.

"And then one day I got a call from Dustin Lee Abraham. He was my best friend and had moved to LA to try his hand at acting. He was using my writing material to audition for parts, and he was succeeding wildly. 'Dude, I just got signed up by William Morris Agency. You should come here and write a screenplay. You'd be so awesome.' 'The William Morris Agency—what is that, a cigarette company?' I seriously had *no* idea about the world he was talking about."

> "I don't like my job, but I love to write," he reasoned. "So why *couldn't* I write a screenplay? Is that so crazy?"

The conversation with his friend kept coming back to haunt him. "I don't like my job, but I love to write," he reasoned. "So why *couldn't* I write a screenplay? Is that so crazy?" The next day he went for a stroll to his local bookstore, intent on buying a few books on screenwriting. En route, he had his second discovery: what he really wanted to do and what he was good at were one and the same thing. He had a sense that not everyone had that advantage, and he intended to do something with it.

That night, Anthony sat down and began writing *The Runner*, his first screenplay. "At page thirty I almost threw it in the garbage. But when I finished it six weeks later, I knew I had something."

Cut to three weeks later—Santa Monica. "There I am, a nobody from Las Vegas, wondering what this producer was doing meeting with me at the end of Pier Three. When I got back to Las Vegas the next day, I kept thinking, Was I out of my mind imagining I could just sell my screenplay like that? Was I desperate and out of touch? But before I could undermine my own efforts, I got a call. 'Kid, this is brilliant. I want to buy it for $35,000.' To me that was a goldmine. I walked into the Mirage, quit my job, and decided to move to LA. But not without the woman who would become my wife and the most important person in my life. I didn't need any stroll to convince me of that decision. We went to LA together. And things took off."

In a few years, Anthony had gone from a tram operator at the Mirage Hotel to a guy who had a manager and a lawyer, three agents at CAA (the hottest talent agency in Hollywood), a contract to write a piece on the Harlem Globetrotters for $250,000, and an offer from Columbia Pictures to purchase *The Runner* for $900,000. It was a dream come true. There was only one catch: he had already sold *The Runner* for $35,000.

"I definitely needed one of my strolls. This time it was more about *rediscovery* than discovery. One million dollars sounded fantastic from where I was coming from. But I've always believed that loyalty is key in business, and I didn't feel right going back on a contract I had committed to. So, in the end, I turned down the $900,000 and went ahead with the small-budget production of the film as originally planned."

Anthony describes the film as a process of "failing upward," but he received the best training in Hollywood film production for the least expensive price possible. The low-budget film allowed him to learn everything about producing a movie firsthand—the setbacks, the barriers, how to deal with actors. Anthony's third stroll wasn't so much a new discovery as a reminder to keep himself on the learning curve. By staying in the discovery mode rather than fast-tracking to the final results mode, he was building equity in himself and in his future. That was going to be worth much more down the road than any high-priced contract he could sign at the time.

Anthony stuck to what he was good at for the next few years, and got a lot of exposure in Hollywood. One day Jerry Bruckheimer Films called, asking if he'd consider writing something for television production. He hadn't been focused on television at all. But it was enticing. The question was, What to write about?

"My wife had been watching a variety of detective shows on cable TV and kept telling me that they had it all wrong. They weren't showing what people really wanted to see. I agreed with her. In a sense I went for another one of my strolls, this time to discover how I might bring life to a world people knew little about. Through a buddy of mine, I arranged to ride with the CSI team in Las Vegas for six weeks. I saw it all—the murder, the violence, the blood, the details of an incredibly important and strange job. I wrote my pitch, confident that I had a real story."

He returned to Hollywood, ready to move forward. After three broadcasters passed on his concept, Anthony wasn't optimistic about the fourth and final broadcaster meeting. As he sat across from Nina Tassler at CBS, he wondered how he could turn this situation around. He was about to launch into his standard pitch, but at the last minute he changed his mind. "Instead, I closed my eyes and just let my monologue fly—a stream of consciousness of what I'd done and seen in the five weeks I was with the CSI team in Las Vegas. I finished and sheepishly opened my eyes. Then I heard the best words ever: 'I love it . . . start writing.'"

And so began his stint with *CSI*, the number-one show that features crime scene investigators as they wend their way through the grisly world of crime scenes in the streets of Las Vegas.

The day of my interview with Anthony also marks the premiere of the spinoff show *CSI Miami*. "I've learned so much on this show, what to do and what not to do, and I know I'll continue to learn as

I move through my career. If you ask me what ambition is all about, it's the story of discovery, rediscovery, and discovery . . . again and again and again."

"What about the fifth stroll of discovery you talked about—when did that happen?" I ask. "Well, that's more of a virtual stroll—it's the stroll I take when I need to find the character's motivation in a script I'm working on; to rediscover what it takes to make a good creative decision; to learn what I need to get to my next level of success; to remind myself why my wife and family are so important to me. It's an endless stroll of discovery that I hope will never go away."

SEARCHING WITH AN OPEN MIND

Whether you're looking to begin a new career or trying to find more meaning and room for growth in the one you've been pursuing for years, discovery—finding out what you do best and what you want to do with it—is the starting point. I define the process of discovery as a state of open-minded "wandering." If you aren't afraid to try out new things or move in new directions, the learning comes easily. The key is openness: loosening up, not limiting yourself, and not censoring yourself—perhaps going where you never thought to go before.

Whether we acknowledge it or not, ambition resides in each of us, be it a little or a lot. Discovery is the key to finding out what your ambition is made up of, what it means to you, and how to bring out the best part of it as you move through your career and your life. Anthony's desire to write and perform and entertain people remained at the core of his ambition throughout his journey. Understanding his ambition came through a constant testing and rediscovery of his talents. For all of us, understanding our own unique brand of ambition makes all the difference between just having a job and knowing that we're pursuing a vocation that brings us pleasure, challenge, and fulfillment.

So how does the ambitionist embrace discovery in a meaningful yet manageable way? There are six key strategies:

Facing your desire Discovery begins with facing up to your desire—an honest evaluation of how you truly define success. This is the starting point of the journey ahead.

Continually asking questions The next and often the hardest part is getting started: igniting the engine that will set you on a path toward learning what you're good at and what you'll do with it. By focusing on the questions and not worrying about the answers, you've already set the process in motion.

Learning the art of spontaneity Set yourself up to take advantage of the unexpected by incorporating enough risk into the equation that you can overcome your fear of the unknown. Embrace spontaneity—and learn how to free fall as a means of gaining knowledge.

Seeing yourself as an apprentice Once you're in motion, the learning aspect of the discovery stage becomes unavoidable. Considering yourself an apprentice allows you to maintain an open mind, to continue learning, and to keep asking the right questions.

Avoiding censorship The biggest barrier to success in the discovery phase is often the creative, intellectual, or emotional paralysis that sets in during the early stages. Learning how to avoid censorship while you're still asking questions allows you to fully explore the many facets of your ambition without having to seek validation along the way.

> **Desire changes and shifts as we change, and since ambition comes from something as powerful and elusive as desire, it has no beginning, middle, or end.**

Trusting your intuitive compass Intuition can be a powerful guiding influence. Find ways to trust your own ideas, even if they're only half formed in this early stage. Allow yourself the breadth of imagination to pursue a number of avenues without knowing exactly what the outcome will be.

Let's look at these six strategies in more detail.

Facing Your Desires

Ambition means different things to each of us. It can mean going after money, power, status, good causes, creativity, fame, new ideas, experimentation, personal fulfillment, or balance. In the discovery stage, ambitionists recognize that desire changes and shifts as we change, and since ambition comes from something as powerful and elusive as desire, it has no beginning, middle, or end. Instead, ambition sneaks up on us and keeps reappearing to challenge our old notion of desire, time and time again.

Rule 1 requires that you face up to what you truly desire—and then continually return to that definition of desire as a benchmark throughout the discovery stage. As best-selling author Harriet

Rubin once said to me, "Desire reframes reality." Nowhere is this clearer than when we're face to face with our ambition. What we desire is based in part upon what we're taught to strive for and in part upon that mysterious element that makes each of us tick according to our own personal meter.

It wasn't until I was consulting with a group of senior executives last year that this concept really hit home. Among these experienced, accomplished people from a host of industries, discussion and disagreement raged about almost every topic that came up. But there was one point they all agreed on: without a means for managing desire, ambition begins to manage you. What does this translate into? For one executive it was the day she realized that she was working for money when what she really wanted was freedom. For another, it was the moment he understood that while he'd been working toward his original goal of CEO at a large firm, along the way his desires had shifted. What he really craved was a chance to test his skills in his own entrepreneurial venture. This group of executives believed that had they been taught to define their desire and continually redefine it along the way, they could have kept their ambition flexible enough to meet their ever-changing goals.

The ambitionist recognizes that by simply engaging in the process of defining desire, the discovery voyage has been launched. The actual definition may come only by working through the next five strategies and constantly returning to the notion that "desire reframes reality." This is part of the open-mindedness that lies at the heart of the rule of discovery.

Continually Asking Questions

To get started, you need to gather enough information to ascertain what it is you do best and what it is you love best. These aren't always the same thing, and that's where asking questions comes into play. Anthony, for example, tried on many different hats before he found one that had the right mixture of creativity and fulfillment for him. He worked as a wire operator (talking, selling), he sold at Merrill Lynch (presenting, performing), he wrote pamphlets while being a tram operator (writing, making money). He was relentless in his pursuit of what he loved, and in his case it happened to be what he was good at. But he allowed himself to ask a lot of questions: What if I were to start working at the Mirage hotel—could I eventually write advertising copy? What if I were to start writing a screenplay—would someone buy it? What if I learned about the strange world of crime scene investigators firsthand—would a broadcaster be interested? What if I gave up a million-dollar gig to learn the ropes on film production—would that help me long term? In other words, rather than allowing his raw ambition to manage him, Anthony designed his ambition to meet his desires. All these questions meant that he was thinking laterally and creatively—and in the process he gained much more than any one "right" answer: he set the stage for his next level of success.

Dr. Clarissa Desjardins is another great case in point. When she was working on her PhD from McGill's Faculty of Medicine as a postdoctoral fellow at the Douglas Hospital Research Centre, during her long hours in the lab she was limited to using radioactive peptides as a way to test cells. Committed to finding an alternative for her own safety, Clarissa created a tool using fluorescents instead. The method proved to be safe and effective, and her colleagues also used it with excellent results. Had she stuck to the job she was given and the research she was assigned, she would never have ventured forward to replace a method that had been used for years.

But Clarissa took her discovery a few steps further. Curious as to why fluorescents had never been used before, she asked questions and discovered that the method had no patent—and so she put the wheels in motion to acquire one. Her sense of discovery didn't stop there. Once she got the patent, she wondered what kind of services she might offer in conjunction with this testing tool. Without any previous training, she asked enough of the right questions to put together a business plan, and eventually, after many setbacks, to establish and successfully run her own company.

But discovery is an ongoing process, and Clarissa continued to ask questions. Would my company be of interest to anyone else? Could I increase its value? As it happened, the biotech world was exploding in the US. After she'd run her company for four years, Clarissa's product and services caught the attention of a much larger American firm, and she sold her company for a substantial sum. Today, she is executive vice president of corporate development at Caprion Pharmaceuticals Inc., a company that applies proteomics to discover and develop innovative products for the diagnosis and treatment of disease. It has raised over US$60 million and continues to grow and expand. Had Clarissa not asked the questions that everyone told her were beyond her academic mandate and beyond her business capabilities, she would never be sitting where she is today.

Like Anthony, Clarissa wasn't only asking the right questions but in the process was challenging herself on two fronts: how deep does my talent go, and how far am I willing to go with it? When setting out to determine both what you want and what you're good at, keep asking the questions that others may try to convince you are beyond your scope. Drive yourself to take on responsibilities that are above and beyond your current mandate and push yourself to find what might seem out of your reach. Even if you never make it past the discovery stage, you've already begun your journey, creating fertile ground for asking more questions regardless of what the answers might be.

Learning the Art of Spontaneity

Not all of us have the luxury of a starting point as specific and focused as Clarissa's. What do we do, then? We go on a fishing expedition, turning to the sport of spontaneity, and we learn how to keep asking questions until something takes. The best way I can illustrate this is to tell the story of Andrew Watson, yet another fascinating individual who works at the top of one of the most inspiring and creative organizations in the world: Cirque du Soleil.

> **When setting out to determine both what you want and what you're good at, keep asking the questions that others may try to convince you are beyond your scope.**

Let me set the stage: I enter the 345,000-square-foot facility that has three acrobatic and two artistic training rooms, a 4,000-square-foot costume shop that produces 20,000 pieces and 4,000 pairs of shoes a year, and that altogether employs nearly three hundred artisans year-round. All of this to entertain the almost 40 million people who have seen the shows at 240 engagements in 90 cities since it began in 1984. The Cirque has 2,500 employees representing 25 nationalities at any one time, so it's no surprise that I'm bumping shoulders with administrative personnel, riggers, trapeze artists, dancers, electricians, and hat makers—all of whom are in line for a well-deserved lunch. It strikes me as a cross between a Silicon Valley campus and a children's playground.

I'm already overwhelmed and the interview hasn't yet begun. Then Andrew Watson, director of creation for Cirque du Soleil, sits down and tells his story. It too is about discovery—the spontaneous kind.

Andrew grew up in the countryside in South Wales, and were it not for his mother taking him to see concerts and plays he wouldn't have had any interest in show business. But this early exposure to the arts was the beginning of a long creative journey. "At seventeen, like most boys where I lived, I left for London to make my way. I had to eat, so I took whatever job was available—I did everything from pumping gas to being an import buyer for a stationery company. I was bored, but I could pay my rent. One day a friend of mine started busking on Portabello Road. He juggled and threw fire and asked me to come along. I did, and despite the fact that I was particularly bad at it, I made money. More important, I liked it. I liked to perform."

That same year, Andrew saw an ad for Britain's Gerry Cottle Circus School and decided to audition. Although, as he puts it, "I couldn't do much but juggle badly and burn myself," he persuaded Cottle to hire him for a program he was launching with a man named Basil Schoultz—a touring show that required five weeks of training before he could hit the ring. The new program would be a revolution in the circus world—instead of the traditional animal and individual acts, a house troupe would perform under one theatrical theme.

"On that first day, I walked into this huge barn where we were to practice and train. There I saw people from all over the world and in every shape and size, all practicing in what looked like a sophisticated playground. I was in awe. In that moment, I discovered what I wanted to do and what I knew I *had* to excel at. I wanted to belong to that world."

Schoultz took Andrew on and trained him well. But life on the road was extremely difficult. "You had to rig your own tents, sleep outside, take cold showers in a bump wagon, and we only made thirty pounds a week, not to mention driving a five-ton truck and cleaning up the garbage after every show. But I loved it. Compared with all the other work I'd done, I'd never been happier."

By 1986 the original troupe of eighteen had dwindled to two. What to do next? Luckily an agent had seen Andrew's trapeze act and entered him and his partner in the Festival mondiale du cirque de demain—a top international industry competition. This was a big deal. "We had been used to playing to small audiences, sometimes only thirty people, in rough neighborhoods where kids would throw stones at us while we were performing. In Paris, we were in front of hundreds of people from around the world for the first time. Suddenly, the world got a lot larger."

They were well received. With offers from some of the best circuses in the world, they decided to join the renowned Circus Roncalli. "Around the same time, I met this man named Guy Caron. He was from Canada, traveling around to all the circuses in Europe with a tent on the top of his car and a rough-cut video of his troupe's performance. Although it was unpolished, it was magical. When I watched it, I thought I saw the future of the circus world. We dined together, I met the other key members of the team, and I guess I caught the Cirque du Soleil bug right then and there. Although our work at Roncalli was wonderful and creative, I felt like I had the chance to join a team that was going to redefine the art of circus performance. It was part intuition and part camaraderie with these guys."

Adopting the art of spontaneity to its fullest, Andrew and his partner decided to take a huge gamble: they left one of the finest circuses in the world to join this small Quebec group that no one had heard of. It was a group that *would* change the art of circuses forever.

"Today, I feel so proud to be part of a team that incorporates so many elements into the act—mask making, dance, lighting, choreography, all to reach and move audiences around the world. I'm so glad that I made my initial journey of discovery and allowed myself to be spontaneous enough to try something as wild as circus performance in the first place. In a way, I never stopped pushing myself until I stumbled onto something that caught my head and my heart. For me, my discovery and my ambition crashed into each other and left me no choice. And I wouldn't have it any other way."

Spontaneity, at its scariest, incorporates the art of the free fall. And that is something in which Andrew is also schooled—literally. He never used a safety net when he performed on the trapeze, an act that could surely result in death or something close to it. "There is a certain confidence," he says wryly, "in knowing that you can't fail, either way." His willingness to risk death in the ring is analogous to the free falling entailed in the discovery stage. You must simply see yourself as a performer who has to eventually make it to the safety of the other side. You keep your mind open, calm and confident that you'll get there because you have no choice. And, in the process, you become skilled at the very act of free falling. You can renew that

> **"I never stopped pushing myself until I stumbled onto something that caught my head and my heart. For me, my discovery and my ambition crashed into each other and left me no choice. And I wouldn't have it any other way."**

skill every time you come to a crossroads in your ambitious journey, every time you need to re-evaluate your desires and your goals. And you get better and better at it.

An associate of mine moved his real estate business from a smaller urban center to New York City, where he was astounded by the differences in the industry. The rules and procedures felt so foreign to him that he found it hard to motivate himself to sell at all. But he decided to simply plunge into the unknown. He lost time and money, but in the process he gained confidence from the fact that he could remain in a state of limbo as long as he kept asking questions. Eventually he discovered a relatively untouched customer niche: the up-and-coming careerists in design, fashion, film, and the arts. Their price bracket was lower than those in, say, finance and business, but since they tended to buy spontaneously the sheer volume made up for the lower price point. And he was also able to minimize his marketing costs, given the effective word of mouth campaign that ensued within this tight-knit group of potential customers. He's sure that neither of these advantages would have come to him had he not put himself into the free-fall mode. He learned a subtle but powerful truth: by simply acknowledging that you're in a free-fall state of mind, you're able to counteract the fear factor in unfamiliar situations.

Seeing Yourself As an Apprentice

Positioning yourself as an apprentice doesn't mean that you have to put it on your business card or your résumé. It does mean that you look for ways to home in on what it is you ultimately want and to fine-tune what it is that you're truly good at. Regardless of whether you get a job as vice president of marketing or in an entry-level position far below your qualifications, determine what you want to learn at this stage of the game and benchmark your success against *that* goal rather than any other. Of course, your professionalism and dedication to any job—corporate, freelance, or not-for-profit—must never suffer due to your private apprenticeship status. But it allows you to remain open to learning and discovery—as any apprentice would.

I know an advertising executive who had years of experience in packaged goods but relatively no experience in the world of politics. Faced with the biggest account of her career for a political campaign, she panicked and didn't think she was right for the job. Why go down that path, stumble, and perhaps diminish her credentials in packaged goods? But after much consultation, we agreed that by seeing this opportunity as an apprenticeship, she could truly throw herself into a learning mode that she hadn't experienced for a long time. She learned a lot about political advertising and PR, and discovered that she had a real skill in this area, so much so that her client encouraged her to move into the political arena. This was an ambition that surely would have eluded her had she stayed committed to her set path.

Avoiding Censorship

Once you've faced your desire, asked questions, toyed with spontaneity, and accepted your role as an apprentice, it's time to apply the simple strategy of avoiding censorship.

Sometimes you know what you're good at, but you aren't quite sure what you're going to do with it. This almost always leads to paralysis as you try to create some kind of game plan before you have enough information to do so. Paralysis is a state we all fall into at one time or another, whether it takes the form of writer's block, stage fright, not being able to sell, or not being able to pull together a good presentation for your boss. The key is to break the censor demons before they bring you to a grinding halt.

When I asked Anthony Zuiker if he ever felt creatively paralyzed, he said, "I go through tremendous confidence swings in the business. Everybody does. You do need validation . . . but more important, you need to keep perspective." We all want and often need outside validation. And that's okay. But if a sense of long-term perspective is missing from the equation, it may lead to paralysis. In his book *Six Thinking Hats,* Edward de Bono notes that "instead of judging our way forward, we need to design our way forward. We need to be thinking about 'what can be,' not just about 'what is.'" Once you commit to being in a discovery mode, almost by definition you'll need to commit to a continual learning curve without reservation and without self-imposed limitations. Here, then, are a few ways to avoid self-censorship.

First, the biggest barrier to beginning is often your own lack of self-esteem. Before anyone else has a chance, your inner voice says, You can't possibly accomplish this. No way, no how. The best way to make headway at this stage is to work *around* the corners of your ambition in order to avoid self-censorship. For example, you want to become a concert singer. Instead of feeling defeated because you tried out for the Met and they turned you down, you could be creating opportunities to sing in other venues, whenever and wherever they present themselves. In this way, you can discover new and unsuspected opportunities as you network and meet new people and other musicians, learn new repertoire, and hone your performing skills. Censorship doesn't have a chance to set in and sabotage your ambition because you're constantly questioning, exploring, and trying out new approaches.

We're often taught to meet our challenges head on, to be straightforward and to take things one step at a time. This can be good advice, but not when it comes to the discovery stage. You can't simply go from A to B to C to achieve success according to your desires—especially when you're still in the process of determining what those desires are. One executive equated the initial stage of the ambitious journey to a sailing regatta: it's often better to take two or three tacks and keep moving toward your final destination rather than sitting on shore wondering aloud what would be the perfect strategy for getting to the end point.

Second, consider the discovery stage as a time to gain knowledge rather than a time to seek external validation. You need to find that voice inside of you that says, I can do this. I may not know exactly where this is heading, but I can do it. This is the strategy that the advertising executive used when she went after the political campaign account for the first time.

Paradoxically, if you have a skill or talent, stick to it. Even if you don't want to continue making your living from it, stay close to what you're good at because having something to fall back on will let you venture farther out on a new limb. The advertising executive could always return to consumer packaged goods and find a way to integrate what she learned in the world of politics into the world of consumer demand. Not such a stretch.

Conversely, and depending on your level of courage, sometimes it's best to explore a variety of ideas, talents, venues, or opportunities at the same time. After all, the discovery mode is all about staying open to unfamiliar territory, and so the more the merrier. For example, suppose you're a writer who works for a newspaper. You feel you need a change, and perhaps you're not even sure what's driving you to change. That's how ambitious ideas often first ignite—with determination *and* with ambiguity. You may want to explore a few avenues, maybe even in another area of newspaper or magazine publishing such as sales or marketing. If you've written newspaper copy successfully, perhaps you'd be good at marketing to the reading public. You may also want to explore the idea of speechwriting—for public speakers, for executives, or for ad agencies. By pursuing both these opportunities at the same time, you'll learn about two completely different vocational pursuits while benchmarking opportunities against each other simultaneously. This allows you to determine what you're good at and what you like much more clearly and quickly. Try it.

Trusting Your Intuitive Compass

There's no denying it: the discovery stage is about a certain loss of control. And for you realists who've probably been squirming in your seats since this chapter began, be warned. You've heard it before, but to gain control of ambition, you first have to allow yourself the freedom to explore. And as with all effective strategies, a counteractive tactic balances this loss of control. It's called the intuitive compass. And the ambitionist relies on it.

The idea here is that you see yourself and your lifework set out on a map with your intuition as the compass. As you make your way through the discovery stage, you'll come across questions you're not ready to ask, ideas you're not willing to accommodate, opportunities you find too threatening. You don't simply dismiss these possibilities and wipe the slate clean; rather, you leave them at the side of the table, at the edge of your personal map, and rely on your intuitive sense for always knowing where due north is, even as you meander east, west, and south. At first this might seem challenging. But once you try it, you'll find that it will become a life skill well worth pocketing.

I worked with a PhD graduate who was highly qualified but couldn't land an academic job for years. He worked in other capacities with the idea that when the time was right, when he could figure out how to break into the academic world, he would re-enter it. After many sessions together, he realized that if he simply began creating opportunities at the edge of what he wanted to do, he would at least begin to home in on the field he was interested in and the kind of teaching position he desired. He began marketing himself as a workshop leader at learning centers and got a lot of experience teaching in non-academic settings because, of course, he was overqualified and an excellent lecturer. In the process, he networked with other professors who were doing workshops on the side and got a much better sense of the kind of work he wanted.

> **Rely on your intuitive sense for always knowing where due north is, even as you meander east, west, and south.**

When an academic opportunity did finally present itself, he hesitated. He realized that by relying on his intuition over the years, he had found a kind of work that he enjoyed and at which he excelled—and he chose to stay on as a workshop leader. Eventually he opened his own learning center that accommodated other professors who found themselves in the same situation he'd been in. Had he not had the confidence in his own intuitive homing device, he might have made a decision based on an old set of desires and forfeited gaining access to his true ambition.

Another way to understand the benefit of the intuitive compass is to think of yourself as leaning into your ambition. Lynda Obst, producer of such films as *Sleepless in Seattle* and *Contact,* calls this "riding the horse in the direction it's going." It's how ski instructors describe your relationship to the moguls you need to navigate—by moving towards them despite the desire to lean back. The natural instinct for all of us is to resist change, to edge away from it. But the only way to truly get through the discovery stage of ambition is to see where it takes you.

A FINAL WORD

Discovery doesn't mean that one day you just walk off your job and decide to do something different. As Anthony Zuiker puts it, "You always need to have a few safe bets and know when to stay safe and secure. But then, be sure to learn to *use* that security as the foundation that frees you to ask yourself a hundred new questions and take a hundred unexpected paths on your journey of discovery."

Andrew Watson is intent on discovery through trial and error. He doesn't believe, for example, that endless schooling is going to help young kids find their ambition or their talent. Because he had to take jobs from an early age, he weeded out what he absolutely didn't want to do, discovered a desire, and then built a skill he didn't even know he had, based on that discovery. That's not often taught in a structured classroom.

Discovery, then, is about deciding whether you're an eternal dreamer or an ambitionist ready to design a journey that will lead to managed success:

- Dreamers can't act on desire, and they shy away from questions that may reveal its demands. Ambitionists set out to ask questions that will uncover what else they need to know in order to face up to their desire.
- Dreamers often learn about their passion but never take the first spontaneous step. Ambitionists learn the art of spontaneity so that they're able to incorporate any opportunities that arise.
- Dreamers visualize being an expert, completing a project, or obtaining a title. Ambitionists temporarily do away with the end result and accept their role as an apprentice on the road to asking the right questions.
- Dreamers need outside validation and allow censorship to guide their notions of success. Ambitionists learn to trust their intuitive compass as a means of weeding through others' definitions of what's possible.
- Dreamers pontificate about the definition of ambition and underestimate the power of discovery as the starting point to creating success in their own mind. Ambitionists recognize that discovery is a catalyst for the betterment of yourself and what you contribute to the world at large, and they use the first rule of discovery to set the stage for the ensuing cycles of ambition.

I asked Anthony, Andrew, and Clarissa how they would describe their journey to date. Anthony Zuiker described his journey as "No limits," Andrew Watson said, "It's the opposite of a roller coaster—it goes up instead of eventually down," and Clarissa Desjardins called it "following my passion."

Like these three ambitionists, if you can begin your ambitious journey with desire and without limitations, you'll be able to explore with the freedom to be surprised and delighted. Know that you've just embarked on a roller coaster that continues to go up and up and up. Once you accept this definition of discovery, you're an ambitionist ready for the next cycle on the journey.

RULE 2
FOCUS

Do not dwell in the past, do not dwell in the future, concentrate the mind on the present moment.
—*Buddha*

What do an adventure racer, theater director, high-tech CEO, and film distributor have in common? The ability to make brave decisions, time and again. And what constitutes bravery? A bias to action. Here's a story that sets the stage for Rule 2 on the ambitious journey.

Robyn Benincasa is the only American woman to win the Eco Challenge and the Raid Gauloises—the two most prestigious adventure races on earth. This is no small feat, given that adventure racers eat Iron Men for breakfast! Imagine a sport where four-person teams are dropped into the wilderness for ten days, during which they must perform specific physical and athletic feats. Not only do adventure racers have to be top-notch athletes; they need to have the mental strength to get through the unpredictable and often life-threatening situations that arise in the wilderness. Robyn is one of them.

"We were in Ecuador in 1998. Our team was in the lead at the crux of the race. It was day three and we had to climb a 20,000-foot active volcano. There was a huge storm raging with little visibility and plummeting temperatures. We'd slept one and a half hours the previous two days and exhaustion had set in. Every team has its athletic strengths; ours was not mountaineering. We got to a particular checkpoint at 15,000 feet where it was mandatory for the doctors to check our oxygen saturation level—anyone below a certain level wouldn't be allowed to continue.

"In adventure racing, in order to finish, the entire team has to participate. Given the extreme circumstances, race officials were allowing one of each team's four members to reach the 20,000-foot mark by giving out a penalty for those staying at the 15,000- or 18,000-foot mark. So there was a lot of strategy to determine how many points a team would lose in ratio to the health of its members.

"At 15,000 feet, my O2 set was 71. Normally, one would be hospitalized for this. I knew I was in trouble because I could hardly breathe. Still, I pushed ahead to 18,000 feet, where I got down on my knees and cried. My lips were blue, but I'd made it and I knew I could go back down for a rest.

"As I began to gather my stuff to return to 15,000 feet, I saw my teammates looking at me. 'Who's going to keep going up?' I asked. 'You are,' they said. *'What?'* As it turned out, one of the other male members of my team was in even worse shape than me. I had exactly two minutes to make my decision: let my team down and potentially lose our lead position or push ahead and risk serious danger? Given my compromised physical shape, it would have been easy to give up, and justifiable to imagine all the 'what if' scenarios.

"Instead, I moved into action and decided I needed to stay with the team. It was decision making at its most dramatic. But being the practical person I am, I knew that more than anything, I needed motivation and moral support. So I asked the French camera team—which was filming the whole race—to come with us. I knew they were mountaineers, and I figured that if I had someone else to watch over us we would at least have some confidence. They agreed. Decision made. We kept climbing.

"It was the most agonizing, slowest three hours of my life. We were literally moving three steps every five minutes. I don't remember most of it because my body was in such shock. But I do remember the French team passing us. As mountaineers, they were looking pretty good. As non-mountaineers, but fierce competitors, we were driven even harder.

"Just before the summit, we broke through the clouds and finally made it to the top under blue skies. It was quite a moment. The race continued at a brutal pace, with four more days of relentless physical and mental challenges. Because we had pushed on, in the end we won the race by two hours. It was the first time an American team won the Raid. It was our goal and we never once lost our focus or determination.

"What I like most about adventure racing is that it's a microcosm of life itself. In ten days or less you're faced with having to survive, maintain your energy and focus, work with a team, succeed, strategize, and, most of all, make one decision after another. It's a series of 'moments of choice' that you face one at a time in order to succeed."

Robyn's story is one of the more dramatic "moments of choice" I've enjoyed firsthand from the many people I interviewed for this book. While each story I heard was unique, they all had a common thread—there's always another fork in the road and a difficult decision to make as a result. This is the norm, not the exception. Your approach, however, is what distinguishes you as an ambitionist.

MAKING BRAVE DECISIONS

There's no denying it—the journey of ambition presents us with interesting yet challenging choices every day. The key is to develop a process to focus on the immediate task at hand while accommodating long-term goals. But here's the catch: ambitionists have to *choose* to step into this arena.

> **There's always another fork in the road and a difficult decision to make as a result. This is the norm, not the exception.**

The perpetual dreamers among us—think of those eternal students who avoid the working world—stay in the discovery mode forever, loosely wondering about the what-if scenarios they play out in their mind. But those who learn how to create a meaningful decision-making process, and how to focus on the immediate next play, will cross over to the ambitionist category. It's that simple. You need to choose to join this group because it doesn't happen on its own.

Building a decision-making process is about finding the balance between consequences: what compromises do I have to make in order to achieve my goals—and results? What will this decision provide for me in the short and long term? By acknowledging the dichotomy that exists between these two realities, and applying some basic decision-making strategies to each fork in the road, ambitionists ultimately find a way to live with the gap. Let's say, for example, that you've just accepted a job that will give you the stepping stones to move into an executive-level position. You have to travel more than you did before, and this will affect your time at home, which is important to you. In order to find a way to live with this, you'll need to reschedule your daily routines dramatically so that you can achieve your end result while minimizing the necessary sacrifices. Not an easy task.

If focus requires a bias to action, then what stops us from making brave decisions more often? The knowledge that these decisions are followed by a lot of hard work and an intuitive understanding that there are no shortcuts. Here, then, are the five key strategies for closing the gap between inevitable consequences and desired results on the road to finding peace of mind.

Finding your pain threshold Sacrifices are part of every decision you make. To determine which decisions will maximize your results and minimize the consequences, ambitionists first determine how much pain they can live with. Only then can they move on to an effective decision-making process.

Making decisions like a trader The focus required in making good decisions time and time again comes from laying out a process that minimizes the emotional elements—establishing a means for analyzing the information and for avoiding decisions that are based on boredom or vanity.

Living with timing The element of timing is an unknown, uncontrollable piece of the puzzle. Ambitionists focus on living with timing to work in their favour—whether that means jumping on an opportunity that others are convinced is before its time or being patient enough to see through a few cycles of trial and error until the ultimate result is apparent. Either way, ambitionists pace themselves so that they don't peak too early on the road to success.

Acting on insight Making a decision in the heat of the moment is often the hardest because the desired result isn't obvious or straightforward. Rather than wait for the perfect opportunity to present itself, ambitionists find ways to rearrange a current situation to meet their own particular needs.

Being an optimistic opportunist This is one of the best ways to minimize the gap between desired results and consequences. How? By creating an opening where others see only barriers, by focusing on the possibilities, and by committing to the end result despite what appears to be overwhelming immediate consequences.

Let's look at these five strategies in more detail.

Finding Your Pain Threshold

Over the last few years I've have had the opportunity to meet and coach a number of salespeople from a variety of industries. Since I myself come from a sales and marketing background, I found that regardless of the industry, many of us had a similar experience when we sold a new product or service. It's called "selling to the pain threshold," and it's a useful concept for launching the focus stage of your journey. Here's how it works.

Let's assume you're selling a new kind of product to the manufacturing industry. As with any sale, the key is to minimize the sales cycle and maximize the potential for repeat sales. What effective salespeople do is determine how their product will solve the customer's specific problem and result in a sale as quickly as possible.

The definition of "pain threshold" in this sales context would be the twentieth time a senior-level executive from a major corporation tells you, the salesperson, that he's going to lose his job if you don't propose a viable alternative to all the money and time his division has been wasting because they don't have your product, or anything like it. In other words, the customer is willing to make a risky decision (buying your new product) in order to avoid the pain he's currently experiencing.

How much pain am I willing to live with in order to move forward in pursuit of my goals? How you answer that question defines your own personal pain threshold.

By spending the time determining where the highest pain threshold lies both within a market and then within an organization, salespeople are able to tap into the most lucrative sales opportunity.

This concept is similar for the ambitionist trying to determine a starting point for making personal decisions. Here the question takes the following form: How much pain am I willing to live with in order to move forward in pursuit of my goals? How you answer that question defines your own personal pain threshold—and will set the stage for the moments of choice you find yourself in and the decisions you need to make.

I found the most wonderful example of this when I interviewed world-renowned Canadian theater and opera director Robert Carsen. His opener: "There's only one really brave thing that I ever did—and of course it changed the course of my life forever."

As you can imagine, this more than made me stand up and take notice. And so I listened.

"I knew I wanted to be in the theater from very early on in high school. I had stumbled into a liberal arts education at York

University and, after failing some auditions to get into Juilliard, I was at a loss as to how I was actually going to 'get' into theater. In my second year, I was sitting in a massive exam room—maybe it was the exam for Romantic Poetry—trying to find some intelligent answer to some esoteric question when I suddenly realized I really didn't care about my answer. As if in a dream, I watched myself stand up, walk up to the front of the class with my exam in my hand, and deposit it in the wastepaper basket. I walked out of the class, got in my car, and drove home.

"My mother said, 'What are you doing home?' and I said, 'I'm going to London tomorrow to audition for theater school.' In that strange moment, I knew I was never going to get anywhere if I stayed where I was. I actually booked a ticket and left the next day.

"After the initial exhilaration of having arrived, I was struck by the fact that I didn't know a soul. And to my utter dismay, I discovered that all the auditions for theater schools were finished. Case closed.

"Bravery, though, has a strange way of changing you. Once I'd walked out of that examination room—it still makes my heart flutter just thinking of it—there was no way I was going to let a simple scheduling issue stop me from achieving my goal. I went to a pub right beside one of the top theater schools and, after hanging out for long enough, eventually met one of the teachers there. He listened to my tale and said, 'What a crazy thing to do. . . . Listen, we've finished with auditions, but you never know. I'll let you do an audition, and if there's any future, I'll see what I can do.'

"In the end, I got into three schools—the Central School of Speech and Drama, the Bristol Old Vic Theatre School, and LAMDA [London Academy of Music and Dramatic Art]. Who would have believed it?"

As Robert paused for a moment, I took the opportunity to scan the extensive résumé in front of me, which included eight productions for the Paris Opera as well as productions for the Vienna State Opera, La Scala Milan, the Salzburg Festival, the Aix-en-Provence Festival, the Metropolitan Opera, and the Liceu in Barcelona. It was obvious that the man is a most accomplished ambitionist.

"It all started with a brave decision and an intuitive sense that to stay where I was would be the very thing that would stop me from achieving my goal. Funny, how that works."

Robert found his pain threshold in a dramatic way. Others come to understand their boundaries more slowly. Regardless, focus on finding your pain threshold and recognize when the need to move on far outweighs the benefits of your current situation. Or, like a salesperson who looks for where and how a product or service will address an urgent market or company need, assess how much pain you're willing to live with in the short run as a means of attaining your desired results in the long term. With this important benchmark in place, you can move on to figuring out a process for making the right decisions.

Making Decisions like a Trader

Decision making is an art. As such, it takes a lot of practice to create a process that will enable you to make the right choices regardless of the circumstances. After I interviewed Simon Franks, chief executive of Redbus, I realized that it comes down to focusing on three important elements.

When Simon decided to go from being a trader at a major investment firm in London, England, to running his own film distribution company, he took all his experience and business acumen with

Decision making is an art. As such, it takes a lot of practice to create a process that will enable you to make the right choices regardless of the circumstances.

him, translating it to a business that was based on a whole other mindset.

"I always knew that I was going to be an entrepreneur. Even as a kid, I was selling bubblegum and soup in the playground to my schoolmates, always looking for a way to make a profit. But when I graduated from university, I knew that I'd need to raise my own capital. So I chose to go into trading because it was the fastest way to make money. By the time I was twenty-six I had paid for my house and saved about three hundred thousand pounds. I had no other obligations and figured I could risk it all—I simply had to figure out what business to go into. The only thing I knew was banking. But since that wasn't an option, I figured I'd go after something I really loved: films.

"To explore film distribution I met with as many industry players as I could in the US, and I was impressed by their professionalism and approach to the business. When I returned to Europe I recognized that there was an opportunity for film distribution on a large scale. I figured that if I could apply the rigor and discipline of the trading floor to the film distribution business, I'd be way ahead of the game.

"I was right. When we began in 1998 we were four people working out of my home. Today we're very profitable and one of the top twenty fastest-growing companies in the UK."

When I asked Simon to describe the trader mentality he applies to his film distribution business, he set out his three basic rules as follows:

NEVER BE EMOTIONAL ABOUT A DEAL

In the film industry, people often buy rights based on emotions. They fall in love with a film and are so attached that it's hard for them to cut loose, even when it's apparent to everyone else that it's not worth it. Simon, however, knows better. "If there's a movie that isn't doing well, I don't throw bad money after good. I cut my losses very quickly. I know from being a trader that you can get it wrong many times. It's just a part of the business. When you apply that to an industry which isn't generally set up that way, it's a winning strategy. To apply this rule, you have to be willing to give any deal up, no matter how far you're originally committed."

CALCULATE YOUR UPSIDE

Yes, there's an element of intuition, a gut feel about a deal. But this doesn't replace taking an objective measure of its possibilities. If you apply sophisticated analysis to a decision, and you make that decision without any emotion, then nine times out of ten you'll be making the right one. One of Simon's latest successes, the film *Bend It like Beckham*, is a case in point. "We spent more money on advertising that film in the UK than on the whole budget of the movie. Many people said we were mad to do it. But we knew, based on our analysis of the data, on our careful and calculated assessment of the potential upside, that the deal had the potential to be worth it. And we were right. Likewise, there have been many movies that we bought the rights to and quickly realized we made an error. Without a second thought, I've ended those deals."

DON'T DO BOREDOM TRADES OR STATUS DEALS

Traders face a lot of downtime—when nothing is happening in the markets. This is when the temptation to start playing the market sets in. But that, says Simon, is exactly when you should leave the office and take a stroll in the park. "You need to have the discipline to move on, move away, and not do a deal out of boredom." Similarly, in the film business, people often do deals based on the status they bring to the table rather than pure business benefits, which is not the way to be successful in the long run.

Living with Timing

Just because we make brave decisions and act upon them in a timely manner, we aren't guaranteed our desired result. We're not, in fact, guaranteed anything. But ambitionists know how to look at their current situation and assess how timing will work for or against their decisions. Let's look at one example from the fast-paced world of high technology.

We used to say, "Remember when we did business without fax machines?" and we impressed ourselves. Today we wonder how we ever got by without the benefit of BlackBerries and Palm Pilots. These devices have allowed us to communicate in real time with anyone and everyone, both within and outside our organization, whether through email, internal scheduling, or messaging. But the high-tech market didn't always assume that personal handheld computing would take off the way it has. In fact, when the creators of the BlackBerry technology first entered the market, it was against all odds that the timing was right.

Jim Balsillie is the chairman and co-CEO of Canadian powerhouse software company Research In Motion. He explains: "In our business, we've defied convention all along. In technology, things go in and out of fashion so quickly. For instance, when we first came into the marketplace, we were betting on wireless data as opposed to paging. At the time, 1997, wireless data was unpopular and paging was in fashion. And if you look back, this thinking isn't surprising because the paging business was bigger than the cellular telephone business.

"The whole world was pushing us to go with paging architectures. But we've always believed in the importance of sophistication of analysis, and in the ability to respect your self-knowledge when making major decisions. So we did the math, we did the physics, and we kept saying that our analysis revealed that paging didn't have the bit rate, the frequency, or the latency. In the final analysis, we determined we had to go with wireless data even though everyone said we were crazy. The funny thing is that even though our product is actually a cellular wireless data terminal, we still call it a 'two-way pager' today. I guess it was our way of appeasing the market while still going ahead with what we believed in."

Jim is quick to point out that throughout their decision-making process, they listened carefully to what industry people were telling them. "We never said no to the advice we were getting with any level of arrogance or superiority, and certainly no emotion. It was more a polite 'no thanks,' and then we stuck to our view of how we saw the market and the timing of how the market would play out. And we were right. Since we launched our first product, people have tried to push us in different directions. But our ability to believe in our own analysis of timing and how the future would unfold has always worked for us."

> "Since we launched our first product, people have tried to push us in different directions. But our ability to believe in our own analysis of timing and how the future would unfold has always worked for us."

What Jim and his team learned is the importance of sticking to your assessment of the situation, just as Simon Franks made upside decisions based on careful analysis. For RIM, it was essential not to follow convention for convention's sake. But more important, they understood that sometimes timing works in your favor and sometimes you simply have to make it work for you. There are no shortcuts to doing your homework and no easy formula that will guarantee the outcome. By simply creating a plan for how to deal with the element of timing, you've put a process in place that might just beat the odds.

Sometimes, of course, the art of timing involves knowing when to be patient and to wait things out. I know of a young man who was CEO of a medium-sized human resources firm that was growing at an incredible rate. After 9/11, the company's planned expansion into Europe fell through and they had to find a buyer. With the right board members on his side, they sold the company to a publicly traded firm with a good reputation. And given the dire market climate at that time, the deal was a good one.

But this CEO had to go from running his own show to playing an executive role within a much larger organization. The frustration of having to deal with bureaucratic processes, along with his inability to make final decisions, began to wear on him. His instinct was to leave, but his training forced him to stay. He knew that the heat of the moment often passes, and that if you ride things out they'll look much different down the road. For about two years he kept a low profile, spending a good deal of his mental energy observing how the company worked and finding the holes in the operation. By that time his division was starting to do quite well, and he had earned a reputation as a reliable team player who stuck it out. With a new sense of purpose and ambition, he was ready to jump back into the game.

He began to make management suggestions and to influence the key decision makers. His salary and bonus had grown substantially from when he ran his own firm, and he was starting to recognize what he liked about working for others. How long this scenario will be of interest to this executive is unknown. But what he learned from the experience was the importance of being patient and of prioritizing. His patience allowed him to simply observe and then to figure out where he could be most effective in the company. And by prioritizing only those things that were within his power to influence, he was able to act upon his decision to stay. In these ways, time was on his side.

Another aspect of savvy timing is knowing when to make your dramatic entrance or exit. Remember the captain of your high-school football team? Everyone wanted to date him—he seemed to have it all. Fast-forward ten years, and he hasn't amounted to much. Or how about the prom queen who never escapes from her image as a teenage beauty? Quite simply, these people peaked too early. Adventure racer Robyn Benincasa's experience in the 2002 Fiji Eco Challenge exemplifies the importance of pacing yourself.

"Despite the fact that we were one of the lead teams, one of our teammates, Mike, got sick with giardia, an intestinal parasite that makes you so delirious and weak you can barely move. Our team had to decide whether to keep going with him in that condition or let him go—and in doing so get disqualified from the race.

"After much debate, we decided to stay with him, get him some rest, and see if we could make up the lost time later on in the race. Magically, we met a few locals who picked him up and nursed him back to health. Despite their apparent poverty, they gave us what little food they had. At this point, Mike was delirious for eight hours at a time and we had to keep waking him up every hour just to make sure he was still alive. At the village pharmacist, we had to decide between local remedies or nothing. In our minds, the race was in the past and the only thing that mattered was getting Mike back on his feet. Miraculously, after six hours he ate and drank, two hours later he started to talk again, and a few hours later he was on his feet and felt ready to go back into the race.

"We were in eighteenth place when two other members of the team came down with the same symptoms, but by that point we knew what to do. And we were just so happy to be back in the race, it didn't matter. In the end, having stopped when we did was what saved us because during the last stint of the race, officials threw in an additional twenty-four-hour hike. Most of the other teams had expended all their energy and had peaked in their performance too soon. They simply dropped out of the race. Out of eighty-two teams that started the race, only six finished. And in that last twenty-four hours, we went from eighteenth to fifth place."

In ambitionist terms, learning how to pace yourself often means forfeiting the temptation of more immediate gratification or gain for the long-term potential upside. This choice enables you to balance end results with consequences, not only in the focus stage of your journey, but as you move through the decisions you'll have to make in the belonging, momentum, and balance stages further along the ambition cycle.

Acting on Insight

By definition, a decision implies compromises. Just as timing isn't always on our side or within our control, how well an opportunity suits our needs can also need massaging. It's all a question of how we look at it. Let's consider an example of how acting on insight can help to focus those moments of choice we all experience.

When we last left Robert Carsen he had just been accepted at three drama schools. Later he directed his own opera, but it was a search that went on for nine years (talk about living with timing!). The next story is about how he finally got his big break, and how he turned the opportunity he needed into the one he deserved.

"There was the internationally acclaimed Opéra de Genève that was run by Hughes Gall and that I always had my eye on. I had met Hughes as an assistant director and approached him, as did everyone, about the possibility of directing a production in Geneva. He said, 'I'll come and see something that you do. But I'm warning you—you better be sure that it's something you really want me to see because I'll only come once.' When I told him the opera I wanted him to see he said, 'No, I don't like that opera. Don't make me come see it—I don't think it's right for you.' But I was excited about the work we'd done on it, so I pushed him to come anyway.

> **Just as timing isn't always on our side or within our control, how well an opportunity suits our needs can also need massaging. It's all a question of how we look at it.**

"He came, he saw it, and . . . he liked it very much. He asked me what opera I'd like to direct. I had planned on giving him a suggestion that I knew few people would put forward—*Mephistopheles*. He was intrigued. He had a particular opera singer in mind who agreed to work with me, and so the only outstanding issue was the design. Because it was a very large and expensive production, he suggested that I work with one of two famous designers to be sure it all went well. And this is where I realized that although I was being handed an opportunity, my big break, it wasn't going to work for me unless I molded it as much as possible to meet my particular goals. I met each of the two designers and realized instantly that it would be a mistake to work for them. I remember ringing up Mr. Gall and saying, 'Look, Hughes, you're giving me my big chance here. If I were to work with one of these famous designers and the show is a success, it would be because of their work. If it's a failure, it'll be because of my work. I'd rather take a chance and choose a designer of my own.' I think he recognized the significance of what I was saying, and amazingly, he agreed.

"In the end, the show was a success and we went on to work together on a number of productions with the Paris Opera, which was really the launch of my career. This year he's doing his last show and has asked me to be the director. An interesting closing of the loop."

Robert not only waited until the right opportunity came his way, but he found a way to rearrange the situation so that he could achieve success on his own terms. In the artistic world, as in many industries, it's not only gaining outside acknowledgment that matters, but also knowing that you've truly dedicated all your talent and efforts toward an original work of art. By upping the ante on his first major opera production, Robert was most definitely raising his pain threshold bar once again. But he was also listening to his own insight that he needed to succeed or fail based on his own merit. Like a true ambitionist, Robert acted on this insight and moved forward in a timely manner.

Being an Optimistic Opportunist

Part of taking advantage of an opportunity that comes your way is focusing on the best possible outcome despite signs to the contrary. We already saw how Jim Balsillie and his team did this at RIM, and we know the strong position of the BlackBerry technology in the marketplace today.

When Simon Franks was faced with the biggest decision of his career, he too had to take a chance and turn it into the break he was looking for. "In 1999 we were still considered a small business. And then an opportunity presented itself to me. Rather, I saw a major change in the industry and jumped on it. Universal bought Polygram for the music business that they coveted. They decided that they didn't really want the film business, and so they subsumed Polygram into Universal. At the time, Polygram was the number one film distributor in the UK with 10 percent of the marketplace, and they simply decided to close it down. It was unheard of. I kept wondering, Why would you do this?

"Through the industry rumor mill, I heard that the staff at Polygram, who had mostly focused on independent films, weren't very interested in becoming a small division under Universal. I smelled an opportunity here—though I wasn't sure exactly what I would do with it. I went to see the managing director of the UK operation, Chris Bailey, and suggested that he come work for us. It was quite a leap, given the fact that we were barely known. But to my surprise he said yes. The only caveat was that he wanted to bring the entire UK business group with him—all nineteen people. Without missing a beat, I said 'Brilliant, fantastic, sure.' And then I went home and panicked.

"At the time, the combined annual salary of our new employees was more than our entire capital base. When I did the math, I could cover one year of salaries

> **Ambitionists can move forward as confident opportunists because of the decision-making strategies they've already put into place to ground them. And in the face of a difficult decision, they never underestimate the power of optimism.**

for this group if I tied up every penny I had. But I realized that this was a one-time gamble—if I was really going to grow the business, I needed the right people in place. I made the move, and we've grown dramatically ever since."

Like other ambitionists, Simon was able to dive into action for two reasons: he had planned for the best possible outcome and he was flexible enough to accommodate the intervening shortfall. Ambitionists, in other words, can move forward as confident opportunists because of the decision-making strategies they've already put into place to ground them. And in the face of a difficult decision, they never underestimate the power of optimism.

A FINAL WORD

Focus isn't just about making concise decisions and knowing how to live with the consequences; it's also about establishing a few key processes and understanding the right mindset that will help you in the ensuing cycles of ambition. In short, it's about learning the ropes and taking it with you as you move on to define success in the world at large.

When I speak with an associate who runs one of the most successful college preparatory businesses in New York City, she always reminds me of the difference between succeeding and learning. There are those kids who learn in order to score high marks but take nothing with them. Then there are those who decide right from the beginning that they're going to take the learning with them after they finish their exams. And that's a key characteristic of an ambitionist. It's not about scoring high marks but learning nothing. It's not about making a decision that looks good but whose consequences detract disproportionately from your quality of life. It's about building a foundation that enables you to learn continuously.

Robert Carson, Jim Balsillie, Robyn Benincasa, and Simon Franks are all ambitionists who have chosen to learn from their own internal decision-making process and to take that learning into the broader world. Making brave decisions implies that mistakes will be made and tougher decisions will ensue. But everyone I spoke to agreed that making any decision is better than no decision at all. Likewise, finding ways to learn from each choice you make is as important as the outcome itself. Brave decisions entail the possibility of error. Error equals learning. It's as simple as that.

RULE 3
BELONGING

Coming together is a beginning, staying together is progress, and working together is success.
—Henry Ford

In a small community in the Yukon, Sheila, a nurse, was preparing to leave after a two-year stint helping out in the local hospital. Her time in this beautiful place had been challenging, interesting, and fulfilling in ways she never expected. She was accepted into a community that was completely foreign to her, and felt that she had truly contributed and was appreciated for her efforts. She packed her bags with hesitation and wondered what she would say at her send-off celebration that evening.

But nothing could have prepared her for what transpired at the little community hall at the center of town. After the food was served, the head of the community came up to the front of the room and, in a somber voice, said: "Sheila, after two years working with us, you have come to be an important part of our life here.

And now we understand that you have to go far away from here and we're not sure when you'll be back. As is customary when a member of our community leaves, we have determined that it's only right for us to offer you the youngest member of our tribe—a newborn baby—to go with you. It's our way of ensuring that you understand you belong to us as much as we will belong to you, despite distance and time."

Sheila wasn't sure she'd heard correctly. But after much discussion, it was clear that in this part of the world, to belong to a community was of utmost importance. In fact, it was essential in maintaining the community's future and the values of the people who made up this distinct group. In the end, Sheila was able to convince the community leader that while she was honored and touched by their offer, she didn't feel she could accept the responsibility of bringing up another person's child.

The next morning, as Sheila looked out the airplane window one last time, she knew she'd never forget the feeling she experienced when she had to compare how much this group of people had come to mean to her with how much she meant to them. Though she put on a good front, the decision wasn't easy. On the one hand, she understood and cherished the finality of belonging, as defined by this community, and envied its unswerving commitment. At the same time, though, it left her wondering where she really belonged.

CREATING YOUR CORE COMMUNITIES

When I first heard this story it struck me that belonging is such an obvious part of the human condition. The paradox about belonging is that it's what we most want and yet what we fight most against. As an international speaker, I'm often asked to talk to leaders and managers about how to find and keep talented people in the company: in short, how to create a sense of belonging that goes beyond a pay check. Anyone who has managed or operated a company is well aware of the struggle between belonging and fierce independence that brand the talented young people they choose to hire. These individuals are trying to determine which company they believe in and want to contribute to while ensuring that they'll be adding equity to their own personal stock in the process. If you're honest with yourself, as an employee you'll likely want to proudly belong to a company, a vision, a product that's worth fighting for. You're not willing to identify with any given company at the price of forfeiting your own personal worth, of course. From both the employer's and the employee's perspectives, belonging needs to be a fair exchange.

Today, whether you're an executive with a large company or a freelance consultant determined to maintain your solo status, the rule of belonging is quite clear. You can't build on your ambition alone and you can't create success without including others. If you don't have an idea that people want to belong to, it's hard to build up enough momentum to gain good clients, rally loyal suppliers, get the ear of the press, and hire the best and the brightest for your team. If you don't have the support of your peers and superiors, it's difficult to carve out a career path that allows you to maximize your strengths and skills while adding income, prestige, and accolades to your résumé. And without the

> **Without the desire of others to want to belong to your cause, your career, and your ideas, there's not much lasting power behind your notion of success, no matter how ambitious you might be.**

desire of others to want to belong to your cause, your career, and your ideas, there's not much lasting power behind your notion of success, no matter how ambitious you might be.

Just as "entrepreneuring" in my first book, *Bulldog: Spirit of the New Entrepreneur*, identified an attitude and stance that anyone could choose to adopt to their work, whether they ever owned their own company or not, the definition of the "ambitionist" in the context of belonging is not exclusive to those who are leaders and executives at the top of an organization. Belonging can be defined in many ways, from what brand you most identify with as a consumer to which kind of people you choose to associate yourself with in order to turn your raw ambition into managed success. You might offer belonging as an approach to encourage others to follow you—as a company leader, as a pioneer within a certain industry, or as an influencer in the world of politics or the media. There's no value judgment of these categories of belonging, but rather a common theme that identifies the ambitionists among us: they find ways to intersect what other people desire with the stories (idea, job description, company, product) they're in the process of building.

Here, then, are the five key strategies for creating a sense of belonging in others:

Defining values Belonging begins with values: most people want to align their values with the brands they buy, the companies they work for, the neighborhoods they live in. By building the value proposition into the messages you communicate to your internal teams and to the external world, you'll help to ensure meaningful belonging.

Choosing your lifeboat team   Success is difficult to generate without the right support team in place. Creating a lifeboat team—a combination of champions, momentum builders, and leveragers—will help you build belonging both within your organization and in the world at large.

Assembling a following   The difference between thinking about belonging to a brand or an idea and actually belonging is the difference between success and failure. Focus on encouraging participation, acting as a catalyst for change within your industry, communicating your ideas in a multitude of ways, and instilling pride in your concepts—all as a means of gaining a true following that lasts and grows.

Deciding on your leadership style   Whether you manage large teams of people or choose to work for others, it's important to determine what your leadership style is so that you can maximize your ability to influence others. By assessing the strengths and weaknesses of four profiles—the warrior, the king/queen, the lover, and the magician—you'll create your own unique leadership approach.

Propelling your team forward   By understanding Patrick Lencioni's five common dysfunctions of teams, and cultivating the correlating leadership qualities that can counteract these potential barriers to successful teamwork, you can create a powerful sense of belonging through team trust, minimizing conflict, fostering commitment, accountability, and paying attention to detail.

Let's look at these five strategies in detail.

Defining Values

Today, regardless of your industry, your ability to create community is what will pave the way for long-lasting success. A certain romanticism has always been associated with the profile of the entrepreneur, the sole proprietor, the free agent who all made it based on their own sweat and tears, but today the trend has swung back to that of partnership, team, and group effort. Over the last decade, the rapid success rate of many high-tech firms upped the ante on the notion of belonging. When stock prices were running high, belonging to your company's brand and being associated with the pulse of the startup you represented were synonymous with your identity. And in a relatively transient society, the company you worked for likely replaced your traditional family structure—it became your neighborhood and you adopted its culture.

For many people, belonging also means choosing brands. Do you wear Nikes or Adidas? Do you drink Starbucks coffee or are you loyal to the local coffee shop? Do you read *Wallpaper** or *Business Week*? It's easy to see why people are attracted to this type of belonging, since it helps them identify like-minded peers.

This notion of belonging is captured in the mock-documentary *Best in Show*, which chronicles the unusual world of people who show dogs competitively. In a scene featuring a particularly high-strung couple who talk about how they met, the woman's account goes something like this: "Well, we were both going to Starbucks—different ones, actually—and we both drank double lattes, and one day we noticed that we were both reading the latest L.L. Bean catalogue. When we actually met and started talking we found out we were both lawyers. . . ." Bingo. Common brands and colliding tastes, however superficial they may be, can function as a starting point for meaningful belonging.

But the real question, once you get past the logo on your shoes or the brand of coffee you drink, is one of values. What, in the end, do you value most? In their book *Emotion Marketing: The Hallmark Way of Winning Customers for Life,* Scott Robinette and Claire Brand talk about the importance that Hallmark places on emotional branding as a means of dealing with consumer complaints. At Hallmark, if consumers had a complaint they were directed to a representative. Then, after they had told their story, the rep would offer to mail them a Hallmark gift certificate.

This sounds fair. But Hallmark found that their approach engendered no emotional attachment. What kind of values was the company communicating—that money heals all and loyalty is bought? And so, by focusing on emotional branding, Hallmark changed its policy. Now when consumers have a complaint they're directed to a senior customer service representative, who asks them detailed questions about the nature of the problem. Then they receive a handwritten apology from that representative in the mail. No money, no gift certificate. Interestingly, the end result is much higher consumer loyalty than when they issued gift certificates. The truth is, people simply want to be valued and want to belong to a brand with upstanding values.

The question of values was really at the heart of this chapter's opening story. Sheila was offered a baby from a small, remote community as an ultimate reflection of how much they valued her contribution. Perhaps, for them, the response to their offering would undoubtedly test how

In determining whom you value, you're setting up your support team, your network that will become a core element you rely on as you move through the later stages of your ambitious journey.

much Sheila valued the community in relation to her own sense of belonging. In a society where people live hundreds if not thousands of miles apart in rough terrain, sharing the responsibility of bringing up the next generation is truly a way to maintain belonging and shared values. When this story was originally relayed to me, it was clear that Sheila almost wished she had no choice *but* to accept the child because that would make her sense of self and identity more concise. But like most of us who live in larger communities, she had a choice, and choice means we have to constantly re-examine our values and take stock of those people we "belong" to before we make any meaningful commitment.

Choosing Your Lifeboat Team

If the notion of belonging begins with the question, *What* do I value? the next question is, *Whom* do I value? In determining whom you value, you're setting up your support team, your network that will become a core element you rely on as you move through the later stages of your ambitious journey.

I once had the pleasure of attending ideaCity, a fantastic, eclectic conference held each year by media innovator Moses Znaimer, the co-founder of Citytv, MuchMusic, and Fashion Television, among others. This conference, which was originated in the US by Richard Saul Wurman, gathers idea generators from around the world and from every industry imaginable. Their presentations allow audience members not only to get a glimpse into the minds of fascinating, enlightening people, but to interact with them as well. At one session, the issue of teams came up. One of the presenters equated the creation of his team with the creation of an inventory of the people he would have on his lifeboat, should he ever be lost at sea. For me, the concept struck a chord.

To get the process started, think of whom you'd have on your own lifeboat team—it should comprise the people you'd turn to when you're theoretically lost at sea. That could be whom you rely on when asking questions in the initial discovery phase (Rule 1), when focusing on making the right decision for your career (Rule 2), or when determining those people within your company who are most supportive of your efforts to generate belonging (Rule 3). Because there are so many valuable attributes and skill sets to assess in choosing your lifeboat team, ambitionists divide their crew into three main categories: champions, momentum builders, and leveragers. To define these categories and their relevance to the notion of belonging, I turn to the story of a top Canadian lobbyist, Adèle Hurley.

As a businessperson your goal is to create success through business deals that generate revenue. If you gain customer acceptance, peer acknowledgment, and press coverage along the way you're delighted, but your essential goal is to create equity and value in your company. Lobbyists, on the other hand, live to influence people, to gain government approval for better policies, and to get people to rally behind them. Their currency is power and influence, and their goal is to better the world—according to their values. Adèle Hurley has been a lobbyist for many years; among other roles, she is the former Canadian co-chair of the International Joint Commission administering the 1909 boundary waters treaty between Canada and the US. But she is perhaps best known for helping to establish the Canadian Coalition on Acid Rain. And when she first started out as a lobbyist, she had to develop champions, momentum builders, and leveragers every step of the way.

After graduating with a degree in environmental studies, Adèle applied her love of the environment to politics, first by working for

Pollution Probe and then as a researcher on the environment portfolio for the opposition leader at the Ontario legislature. While looking into all kinds of concerns—from PCB levels among women living in the Great Lakes Basin to the liquid industrial waste problem in and around Hamilton—she started to read about something called acid rain. It was 1979 and, although the Swedes were writing about acid rain, little was known about it in North America. It was clearly as much of an issue for Canadians as it was for Americans—truly a lobbyist's dream.

After speaking to the Federation of Canadian Naturalists, Adèle was chosen by her peers to go to Washington as the catalyst for the Canadian Coalition on Acid Rain. She didn't have a single lead, but she did have the presence of mind to follow her instincts. The Reagan administration had just come to power and it was clear that the views of environmental groups weren't going to be a top priority. So, as a starting point, Adèle focused on the producers of pollution abatement equipment: a commercial interest, in other words, versus a purely environmental one. It was through her drive and tenacity that she was granted a Sunday afternoon meeting with John Adams, the head of the PR firm that worked for these producers.

"So there I was, sweltering in the ninety-five-degree weather reading my Sunday *Toronto Star* outside his office, wondering what I would say to him. As it turned out, not only did this group reside in the heart of the lobbyist row at Eighteenth and K Streets, but it turned out this gentleman was originally a Brit. When he saw a picture of the Queen Mother on the front cover of the *Toronto Star* that I was holding, he melted, and after recounting tales of his service in England, he instantly became my champion. He offered me office space, and the use of all of his industry publications as well as the AP ticker [access to all media coverage]—I was suddenly a lobbyist in business. From that moment on, I was able to build a viable organization in and around acid rain which crossed borders."

And that's how Adèle starting to build the lifeboat team that allowed her to leverage her lobbyist capabilities. Let's look at how she created her three categories of team members.

> "You have to have mentors in this business. You must find people who have more experience than you and are willing to give you that extra bit of help that can make the difference between getting your cause up and running and struggling to survive long enough to be heard."

CHAMPIONS

These are the people who defend a person or a cause. Inherent in this is an emotional attachment, a commitment that's maintained through various decision-making processes. Champions are those who provide moral support. They can include friends, colleagues, and, in particular, family members. And they're the people you turn to when you need to make a decision or work out a strategy for your next viable ambition. Adèle developed champions throughout her career, which is part of a lobbyist's job. But one of her most important champions was John Adams. "You have to have mentors in this business. You must find people who have more experience than you and are willing to give you that extra bit of help that can make the difference between getting your cause up and running and struggling to survive long enough to be heard." Adams gave her just that kind of support, and once she got going, he became an important, albeit hands-off, sounding board. And when Adèle moved on to lobby for other different causes, this model of a champion, or mentor, would be repeated many times throughout her career.

MOMENTUM BUILDERS

These are the people who move within the spheres of influence that relate directly to your business or personal goals. They can influence other relationships; help you sell your product, talents, or ideas; and help you fine-tune the messages you communicate about your company or line of work. For Adèle, getting Canadians behind the Coalition on Acid Rain became crucial to her survival in Washington. It was an expensive endeavor to support one full-time person living and working in the heart of Washington, and despite their best efforts to raise money for the cause, it was a struggle. That all changed when Adèle had the chance to be interviewed by Adrienne Clarkson, who was a CBC reporter at the time. Clarkson asked a lot of probing questions, and Adèle was frank about the challenges she faced. Little did she know that once back in Canada, Clarkson spread the word, which greatly assisted the group in its fundraising efforts. That's the sign of a momentum builder.

LEVERAGERS

Those who are closest to the revenue line are the ones who can help you put your existing skills, service, or product out there in the world in a profitable way. They can include your sales force; the agent who sells your literary, acting, or athletic talent; or simply a long-standing supplier. The leveragers whom Adèle relied on most were the staff at all the government and lobbying offices in Washington. As she put it, "The most important rule for lobbying is to make friends with congressional staffers, the people who, like you, didn't necessarily have names that mattered but were your entry point to those people who did matter. I'd always get them the information they needed on time and follow up to ensure that it was what they wanted. I was their foot servant, their gofer. In the end, these were the same people who provided me with the information I needed and became my point of leverage with the top influencers and decision makers."

Ambitionists take the time to assess and reassess each of their champions, momentum builders, and leveragers to see if they're "current." You need to ensure that there's a two-way loyalty between you and your lifeboat members—as Adèle did in her ongoing communication with staffers across the board—but you also need to continuously ask if these people understand and support your current definition of ambition. Just as a company needs room to mature and evolve, so do ambitionists and their lifeboat teams. Sometimes certain champions, momentum builders, or leveragers can become a barrier to your success, and it may be time to turn over the makeup of your team. Says Adèle: "People always refer to the saying 'You are what you eat.' Well, you're also who you associate yourself with. It's important that you always have true champions around you who reflect your current beliefs."

Assembling a Following

Once you've defined the value of belonging and established your lifeboat team, the next important strategy is to get the world to *want* to belong to what you do, sell, or create. To illustrate, I turn to the world of design. Design, after all, is an integral part of how we live, entertain, dress, and adorn ourselves. What better example of belonging than the people who create the spaces, fabrics, and clothes that we yearn to identify with?

THE PARTICIPATION FACTOR

Belonging may begin with observation ("Do I *want* to belong to that brand, idea, etc.?"), but it ultimately depends on your decision to participate ("I choose to be part of the community around this brand, idea, etc."). And it is this participation that defines the approach of the renowned fashion designers Dan and Dean Canten behind D-Squared. Having recently won the Man of the Year Award for GQ and the Fashion Oscare de la Mode in Italy, D-Squared is a highly coveted fashion label worldwide and has attracted such major pop stars as Madonna and Ricky Martin. Let's look at how these ambitionists got to where they are today.

The Canadian-born identical twins were always fascinated with clothing, shoes, and accessories. Becoming fashion designers was a dream job they thought was out of their reach, but when they were sixteen Dan and Dean took a fashion course at Parsons School of Design and were lucky enough to find a large manufacturer in Canada who recognized their talent. They ended up designing for this company for six years, and when the company changed hands they knew it was time to move on. Although the twins had acquired a nice house and all the trappings of early success, they wanted more. And to get it they'd have to go where the international plays were made: Italy.

"Everyone around us thought we were crazy to give up what we had," says Dean. "But in a way it was part of our upbringing. When we were little, our dad would throw us into the deep end and say either swim or sink. We knew we were destined to swim then, and I guess that's how we saw our fashion career years later."

Dan and Dean didn't have an easy time of it at first. Without having trained at one of the big houses like Prada they couldn't get a job anywhere, and so they used their own money to make a line of men's clothing for a show in Italy. But when the organizing team saw their samples, they said their clothes weren't right for the show. The twins, who had spent every last penny on the samples, were determined to have something to show for it. With a lot of legwork and last-minute planning, they ended up selling at the Men's Apparel Show in Paris. To their delight, they had sales of over five hundred thousand dollars at that one trade show. And that's how they got started on their own label.

The key to Dan and Dean's success is that their designs have never taken advantage of a new trend or been based on any esoteric idea of what people would like. Instead, they create clothing lines that stem from the needs and desires of their own lives and those of their friends and associates. As Dean says, "We like to go clubbing, so we'll create a line of shirts and pants that work in that environment. Or, one time we had to go to the opening night at the opera and we realized there was no tuxedo we'd want to wear, so we decided to design a tux and it became a part of our line of clothing. I think this authenticity and our own participation in our work is what makes people want to wear our clothes."

This same approach extends to the way Dan and Dean treat the models who show off their clothes on the runway. "In this business, models are often hired to wear the clothes the way the designer and the stylist think would be best for the show as a whole. But we don't do that. We ask models to come in and choose which clothes they like best. If they love to show off their bodies, why not let them model the bathing suits? If they feel comfortable in more formal clothes, let them do that. In the end, they feel great, the clothes look better on them, and they have a great time. This only works to help extend our brand in the marketplace."

The kind of participation that Dan and Dean are talking about here echoes Adam Smith's economic principle of enlightened self-interest, whereby, in Smith's words, "It is not from the benevolence of the butcher, the brewer, or the baker, that we expect our dinner, but from their regard to their own interest." It's a notion of participation that Adèle Hurley has used to build her entire career. That fish could die in the Great Lake Basin, for example, was highly germane to the tourism industry there. By couching her fight against acid rain in terms that were relevant to people's immediate interests, Adèle was able to raise support. And, of course, this concept of participation is no stranger to marketers worldwide. Iams dog food, for example, understands belonging and uses it to target its market very specifically. How? When the company has a special mail-in rebate, they ask recipients to answer one question: "Do you give your dog a Christmas gift?" If the answer is yes, then most likely this person belongs to Iams' brand profile in that they put time, money, and emotional investment into their dogs. And, chances are, they'll pay more for their dog food.

> **Whatever industry you work in, find the entry point that will encourage participation. Target your audience wisely so that their kind of participation and the level of choice they have to make meet their desire to belong.**

Whatever industry you work in, find the entry point that will encourage participation. Target your audience wisely so that their kind of participation and the level of choice they have to make meet their desire to belong. Dan and Dean communicate choice to their models differently than they communicate their hands-on approach to the media; Adèle communicates environmental issues to stakeholders in the travel and tourism industry with a different spin than when she communicates with staffers at government organizations. And focusing on the participation factor immediately sets you apart—you're not afraid to get your hands dirty in the product or service or career you're building. You're open to input from others and welcome their choice to belong to what you've created.

CATALYSTS FOR CHANGE

Artists and designers work to challenge and expand our sense of beauty with new ideas and perspectives on the world in which we live. In a sense, their role as catalysts is as important as their role as artists.

Karim Rashid is one such catalyst. Born in Egypt and raised in Canada, he studied industrial design at Ottawa's Carleton University before going on to graduate studies in Naples. He's taught at Philadelphia's University of Arts, the Rhode Island School of Design, and the Pratt Institute in New York. As a child, he was always fascinated with things that made up the real world—alarm clocks, glasses, cups, lawn mowers—and spent hours drawing everything he could get his hands on. For him, it meant "finding refuge in the manmade physical world" based on "a fascination with what the masses used every day."

Whether it was *The New Domestic Landscape* exhibit that he saw at New York's Museum of Modern Art in 1971 or the vacuum cleaner that could vacuum itself designed by Buckminster Fuller and shown at Montreal's Expo 67, Karim was drawn to the field of industrial design from the get-go. After years of working for an industrial design company in Canada and then going on to teach at the Rhode Island School of Design, Karim eventually found that he wanted not only to design beautiful, useful things for everyday life, but to change the context for how these consumables are viewed.

"I lived on the floor of my brother's apartment in New York City and took trains and buses across America, approaching every company that I thought needed help in designing their products. I wasn't only interested in telling them how to make their product look better and sell better; I wanted to show them how they needed to look at their product as part of a bigger world. For example, if your company makes kettles and only worries about kettles, then there's no context for how the kettles are going to be used. Maybe it's not only for boiling water, but part of the social structure of inviting people over for tea, or wanting to use the kettle to serve, not just to boil water. I wanted to show clients how to design a vision, a future, and a way to move forward from a manufacturer to a provider of designed products for real-life issues."

Karim's version of designing for real life didn't fly with ninety-nine of the companies he approached. The hundredth company was a designer-products manufacturer called Nambé. "There was one new guy in marketing who saw potential in my rhetoric and gave me a chance. The line we did was very successful, and in a sense that was the beginning of my design firm. Since then I've designed products and spaces for over five hundred companies around the world. And in each case, I still see myself as a strategist and a catalyst who works with everyone from engineering, distribution, marketing, shipping, and technical support. In that way I get rigorous insight into a company and help them change their vision of the future."

Not all of us are willing to take on the challenge of designing the future of the companies we work for or the careers we carve out for ourselves. But it's still important to find a single opening that allows you to create change as a way of getting others to belong to your cause. If you work in the administration department of a company, look for ways to save money that may also create a sense of camaraderie among employees; if you work as an assistant in a marketing department, make suggestions that will not only help your superiors manage time and resources but may also reveal a new way of looking at marketing projects that could motivate and inspire. Being a catalyst, whether in a grand sense or not, differentiates you and allows you to expand your ambition.

Taking on the role of the catalyst can be achieved in a variety of ways, and it's important to find a mode of encouraging change that's akin to your particular style.

Think of the kettle manufacturer who, rather than focusing only on how to ensure the water boils within a certain amount of time, understands the importance of recognizing how his kettle will be used in the homes of millions of people around the world.

Taking on the role of the catalyst can be achieved in a variety of ways, and it's important to find a mode of encouraging change that's akin to your particular style. One approach that many ambitionists use is to focus on the notion of "good times," or what's referred to as the "comfort factor" as a means of gently cajoling people out of their routines and trying new ideas. Tricia Guild, the force behind the UK company Designers Guild, is a perfect example of this kind of catalyst.

Designers Guild is known worldwide for the luscious furnishing fabrics, wall coverings, upholstery, and bed and bath collections it produces. In addition to running an international organization of more than two hundred employees, Tricia has authored several highly acclaimed books on everything from flower arrangement and home decorating to color usage. It was a wonder I was able to get twenty minutes with her on the phone.

"What fascinates me is creating lifestyles for people that they feel they belong to, if you like. And so I'm always trying to provide the comfort factor—through my books, my design, a new collection, or whatever. It's my way of being part of their need to belong and a way to help them create an environment that reflects their individuality.

"With designing spaces, there's always the fear factor. Even if you choose white, it's not an easy option. My approach to color and texture allows people to pick and choose what makes them feel most comfortable by creating an environment that's perhaps a little more challenging than what they first set out to create. In the challenge, there always lies the sense of satisfaction and, ultimately, creativity. The result of my work is that I try to make people identify with color, texture, and the combinations, then choose to belong to them."

Like Karim, Tricia has always been attracted to design, but in her case she "just desperately wanted to create beautiful fabrics and keep house." Whereas Karim helps his clients see how their manufactured goods fit into a larger vision of "everyday design," Tricia encourages her clients to broaden their definition of creativity without asking them to abandon their comfort zone. Both work as catalysts for creativity, change, and a new sense of belonging.

PLURALISTS' BROADER APPEAL

In the pursuit of creating core communities, you need to determine whether it's to your advantage to focus in on a specialty or to maintain the stance of a generalist. Do you commit to being the best possible speechwriter, for example, or do you create a personal brand around your writing ability and sell yourself as a marketing strategist with many specific talents that include speech writing? Do you establish your reputation as a biotech researcher or do you evolve your understanding of biotech innovations and focus on your ability to do business development for a pharmaceutical firm?

From the research I've conducted over the years, I've learned that being a pluralist bodes better for creating belonging. That's because pluralists take risks in different areas and build up their ability to accommodate these experiences. Consequently, they're able to relate to both specialists and generalists within their field and spend their time and energy building a platform that's an attractive place of belonging for a much broader audience. In the end, this enables pluralists to build brands and create loyalty. Again I turn to the design world to illustrate the importance of pluralism.

Karim Rashid is, of course, a designer by trade. He's best known for his industrial design of the Oh Chair and the Garbo Trashcan for Umbra, the Kissing Salt and Pepper Shakers for Nambé, and the Morimoto restaurant for "Iron Chef" Morimoto. But he's also launched a CD, written many articles and publications, and collaborated on a fashion line in Paris. Not only does his ability to attract people increase dramatically by extending his reach, but with each new project he becomes better able to help his clients understand how their products might fit into the bigger picture.

This same approach to design is used by Kate Spade, accessories designer and co-founder of her self-named company. When asked about her strengths as a designer, she responded: "We had one big advantage when we started our company—neither [my husband nor I] came from the fashion design industry. We didn't take our cues from the design industry; we took our cues from customers."

Tricia Guild is a pluralist in a different way. She travels the world extensively and looks for ways to incorporate the works of various cultures and specific artistic and craft elements into her own work. Tricia has found a way to blend the influence of Eastern decorative art, Italian Renaissance architecture, and influences from India, Morocco, and every part of Europe. She also incorporates the works of such artists as Howard Hodgkin, Janice Tchalenko, Michael Heindorff, and Kaffe Fassett by translating their imagery from the canvas to textiles. Incorporating all of these cultural and artistic influences immediately broadens the Designers Guild appeal and heightens the desire to "belong" to a design aesthetic that encourages such variety.

PRIDE OF OWNERSHIP

When it comes down to it, people want to identify with a brand, company, idea, or design concept because it makes them proud. From the engineer who's proud to be part of a team that changes the way engines work on a plane, or the human resources executive who helps to implement a new policy for hiring practices in a tough industry, to the end user who's proud to show off his new living room design based on the Designers Guild's new collection, belonging requires pride of workmanship.

When it comes down to it, people want to identify with a brand, company, idea, or design concept because it makes them proud.

Karim explains it this way: "When I work with a client, ultimately I try to convince them that they have to do something that they're proud of. . . . Why not make something that can be referenced on your tombstone—something that lasts?"

Kate Spade talks about her pride in the way her company regards its customers. When asked how she creates a passionate following among people who have too many choices, this was her reply: "For one thing, by treating customers well. Simple politeness has become a lost art—especially in the fast-paced fashion industry. That's why, when we hire people, we give them a copy of Emily Post's *Etiquette*. We remind our salespeople that customers are spending their money with us and that we should show our appreciation. That sounds obvious. But the more popular you become—the hotter your products become—the easier it is to forget such a basic principle. And as important as it is to treat customers with respect, it's even more important to respect what they say."

Finally, Tricia Guild talks about simply "making it right." Pride is what inspires her to strive to live up to her own standards in everything she does. "I see all the work I do as work in progress, and as such, I have to do it right every time—from the flowers I choose for my table and the postcards I send to my friends to the products I create for my customers."

Regardless of how each of these designers look at their work, they recognize that the need and hunger that motivate people to constantly improve and strive for more are the crucial ingredients that will generate the next big idea, and, in turn, keep people coming back for more. To fully maximize belonging, everyone needs to recognize his or her style and approach to influencing others—not only in pursuit of creating belonging, but as a means of laying the groundwork for the subsequent rules of ambition.

Deciding on Your Leadership Style

In order to build belonging into your ambitious journey, it's crucial to understand the significance of different leadership attributes and to develop a leadership profile that suits your own unique attributes. You may not see yourself as a leader, or you may not choose to be a leader in the traditional sense of the word. But whether you lead or manage people in a more structured format or whether you simply need to motivate and guide them along the way as a means of creating success on your own terms, you'll still want to cultivate your own personal style of influencing others—a skill that's necessary for all ambitionists.

In grappling with this question of leadership styles I came across Robert Moore's *King, Warrior, Magician, Lover: Rediscovering the Archetypes of the Mature Masculine*. As it happens, the four archetypes that Moore outlines in his book work equally well as profiles for leadership and influence. The point here is not whether you fall into one of these categories or another, but rather to choose the best qualities exemplified in each of these profiles and incorporate them into your leadership style to best suit your cause.

Here, in a nutshell, are the four leadership profiles:

THE WARRIOR

The warrior is the kind of leader who is attracted to high stakes and risk, whether in the name of an altruistic cause, a creative project, or the launch of a new product. Warriors enthusiastically throw themselves into the fray and love to win. Their strengths include an ability to deal with high-risk situations with a very cool head, a readiness to confront conflict or potential barriers, and good problem-solving skills for big-picture issues. The warrior's weaknesses are an attraction to high stakes at the risk of long-term gain, a tendency to see the world in black-and-white terms (winners and losers), and less than attentive management skills (not detail oriented).

THE LOVER

The lover is the great influencer, the one who can get you to fall in love with an idea, product, or design. They're good managers who appeal to people on an emotional level while maintaining a certain amount of pragmatic toughness. Among the lover's strengths are a highly developed intuition, strong conceptual skills, an ability to think laterally rather than linearly, and an ability to keep a team working together. On the other hand, lovers can be prone to playing politics, to letting their emotions override their rationality in decision making, and to being fickle in their likes and dislikes.

THE KING/QUEEN

The king/queen is the epitome of the diplomat: someone who can take disjointed groups of people and figure out how to get them working harmoniously together. The king/queen is fair and maintains a degree of detachment. These people rise to leadership roles in times of duress and conflict, are able to listen well without being swayed, and bring out the best in others. They can also appear remote in their dealings with team members, lack spontaneity, and be process and structure oriented sometimes to the detriment of the overall solution.

THE MAGICIAN

This is the archetype of the entrepreneur, the dream maker who can draw other people into the story almost by the power of his or her personality and vision. Magicians are strong leaders because they can get people to follow and remain loyal to a concept better than anyone else. They're eternal optimists, and they're able to change direction and reverse important decisions without hesitation. Magicians' weaknesses include a lack of attention to detail, little interest in team structure and process (looking for pure results), a tendency to use force of will to override others' judgment without knowing it, and a capacity to alienate followers.

In order to assess your leadership style accurately, focus on the following questions as you review each of the above profiles: Which profile am I most attracted to? Which profile am I most afraid of? Which strength do I admire most? Which weakness am I most threatened by? Who do I know that epitomizes each of these profiles, and do I admire them in their successes?

Once you've honestly answered these questions, one of two observations may occur. You may find that you squarely fit into one profile or another and can imagine finding ways to maximize the strengths of that profile and minimizing or compensating for the noted weaknesses over time. Or, as many do, you might find that you're a combination of two or more profiles and can honestly sketch a leadership profile that reflects a combination of traits (good and bad) and is uniquely your own. What's most important is your honest assessment of your style of influence.

> **Assessing your style of influence is a first step in understanding how far you can go in creating core communities. But it's important to link theory and reality; to compare the profile on paper to the actual teamwork.**

Once you've done that, you're ready to look at ways to incorporate the best of each of the leadership styles as it relates to teamwork while maintaining your own unique version of leadership.

Propelling Your Team Forward

Assessing your style of influence is a first step in understanding how far you can go in creating core communities. But it's important to link theory and reality; to compare the profile on paper to the actual teamwork. I found a wonderful starting point for this exercise through a speaker and author with whom I shared a podium a few years ago. Patrick Lencioni, in *The Five Dysfunctions of a Team: A Leadership Fable,* applies his unique storytelling style to describe the five most common barriers to effective team productivity and cooperation: absence of trust, fear of conflict, lack of commitment, avoidance of accountability, and inattention to results. It struck me that by correlating the leadership profiles I outlined above to each of Lencioni's five areas of dysfunction, ambitionists can more readily practice their leadership skills. Ultimately, they can determine if they have what it takes to be a leader, or if they might better influence others one on one.

MINIMIZE ABSENCE OF TRUST

Most of my interview subjects said that leadership begins with self-knowledge. As one software executive put it, "A good leader has gone through a pretty rigorous self-assessment exercise. I know for myself, I keep a list of my weaknesses and strengths in my car and at my desk, and I check in on them regularly. If I start to feel that any of my weaknesses are getting out of balance or I notice a new one rearing its ugly head, I'll be the first to take action. I've found that in doing this, in recognizing that I'm not perfect and admitting to my faults, I'm able to break down any unrealistic aura around the untouchable leader profile. And I think my people have come to depend on this kind of honesty." Not believing your own bullshit sets a realistic benchmark for the other team members. Everyone has a set of non-strengths, and admitting to these allows your team to build trust in you as a leader.

Trust is also the basis for making good team decisions. Team members know they can voice an opinion and not fear humiliation if it reveals a personal weakness, and leaders know that their colleagues will tell them when their ability to listen is slipping through the cracks and hampering team progress. As one consultant put it, "You know what you know, and you know what you don't know, and you don't pretend you know what you don't know." Surround yourself with people who have legitimate power and authority to call your bluff, and ultimately you'll be able to make better, more timely decisions.

In order to accomplish this effectively, you may choose to take on the best qualities of the magician. While you may be working very hard behind the scenes to ensure that team members have what they need to complete the process themselves and take ownership of the decisions made, you can find ways to foster an atmosphere of loyalty—and maybe a little magic—in the way the team works together.

MINIMIZE FEAR OF CONFLICT

Theater and film directors always refer to what a character "wants." What does one character want from another character? What does one character long for more than anything? In the world of drama, without wanting, nothing happens on stage or on the screen—it sets up the conflict and potential for resolution. This same tension is necessary in the working world. Everyone has secret desires, agendas, and—to bring it back home—ambitions. As a leader, it's much more productive to assess your team members' inner ambitions at the outset than to be surprised when they arise at an inopportune time. Just as a director knows what one character wants from the other and works with both actors to show how that desire will be resolved, it's the leader's job to anticipate the ambitions of his team members and find a way to accommodate them.

Designers Dan and Dean of D-Squared, for example, occasionally have to deal with an agent canceling a model at the last minute before one of their shows. This can be extremely disruptive, but instead of getting thrown off course Dan and Dean always have a backup plan in place. They know that everyone has his or her own agenda, and it's their way of recognizing that leadership requires a work-around plan to accommodate this potential for conflict.

Conversely, to ensure that your team members aren't hiding their true ambitions because they're afraid they may create conflict, ambitionist leaders find ways to expose those ambitions in a positive light and use the energy behind them to propel the team ahead. Think of the king/queen profile at play here. The lobbyist, for example, rather than battling for the same limited power, keeps all her interested parties moving forward by constantly asking for their agenda and assuring them that it can work in parallel to what other groups are fighting for. Similarly, the designer finds ways to get his team to work together on something new so that everyone gets a fair share of personal credit without undermining the integrity of the overall project.

Ambitionist leaders also need to know how to discern when a team is no longer working well. The people I interviewed for this book pointed to some obvious behavioral signs: team members who don't return messages, who avoid eye contact in meetings, who stop laughing and joking with each other at meetings or in social settings, and who appear to be looking for a new place to belong (i.e., a new job) while guarding their customer and supplier relationships from the rest of the team.

Looking for these signs usually provides enough runway to get to the source of the problem and re-establish some rules of engagement that will speak to the various individual desires and goals. But there are, of course, *some* personal ambitions that won't mix with those of the team or company, and in this case it's essential that the individual leave, quickly. Knowing when to let someone go is often a lot harder than knowing when to hire someone. But by taking on the detached, decisive profile of the king/queen, leaders can assess both individual ambitions and group productivity and determine when it's appropriate to make a move.

> **Only a true leader can rally the team and put the collective good ahead of personal desires. Just as you name your own ambitions, you need to allow your team members to do the same.**

MINIMIZE LACK OF COMMITMENT

Only a true leader can rally the team and put the collective good ahead of personal desires. Just as you name your own ambitions, you need to allow your team members to do the same. As a result, you enable them to be who they are and support them for their specific contribution. However, just as the members of an adventure racing team each have their own personal ambitions, it's the ability of the team to pull through each step of the race as a unit that allows them to make those strategic decisions that will put them in a lead position. And it's no different in the design, film, finance, or lobbying worlds.

A screenplay writer admitted to me that he once became enamored with some of the actors in the movie he was working on. Rather than associate himself with the other writers who were working alongside him, he began to hang out with the celebrities and listen to their input on script changes. Ultimately, the celebrities got tired of him and stopped confiding in him, and when he tried to get back in with the other writers he wasn't well received. His team felt that he had snubbed them and that his loyalty had shifted. Eventually, he was able to regain their trust. But the experience taught him to never again underestimate the importance of team commitment.

The ambitionist leader who acts as a warrior is best able to counteract any lack of commitment. The warrior constantly focuses the team on group success through group tactics, much like that required in battle. By focusing on the *we* instead of the *I*, team members can find a way to live with the reality that their individual success ultimately depends on group achievement.

MINIMIZE AVOIDANCE OF ACCOUNTABILITY

So much of a leader's job is to be the conductor or architect and create patterns between people, places, and opportunities that will maximize the number of good decisions the team can make. By embracing the profile of the lover, ambitionist leaders focus on taking a back seat to the decision-making process as much as possible. They allow others to become the heroes by guiding them to make the right decisions. Inherent in this is a true love of helping others to succeed. If you subscribe to the principle of hiring people who are smarter than you, guiding your team members to do what they're eventually going to learn how to do on their own is a truly noble way to lead. And along the way, you foster in people a willingness to be accountable for their decisions.

Some leaders use terms such as "shared destiny," giving team members a way to differentiate between company and personal goals as a basis for decision making. Others simply provide support when they're asked. But most successful leaders eventually recognize that if all important decisions are made only by the top sphere of executives, the company is greatly limited in its potential to grow into new markets. There is, after all, only so much time a handful of decision makers have in a day. But when a team is built on accountability and decision making is a *requirement* of team participation, the potential for growth filters up through all levels of an organization. One executive puts it like this: "I've always found that good, bright people drive themselves harder and better than any one leader can possibly manage to do. I always give my team independence, accountability, visibility, and trust. I've rarely been let down." In short, the ambitionist leader who works to support decision making at all levels of the team minimizes the avoidance of accountability.

MINIMIZE INATTENTION TO RESULTS

While ambitionist leaders always keep their eye on the big picture, at the same time they make sure to pay attention to the details. "You have to have a certain level of fidelity to excellence or 'specialness,' an unrelenting desire to search for 'better' in every element of your business," notes Tricia Guild. "Whether that translates into how you delight your customers, pay heed to the layout of your offices, or focus on the quality of your workmanship and the timeliness of your marketing, there's no substitution for that attention to detail which, in the end, gives you the kind of results that you and your team all live for."

Each of the four leadership profiles can encourage this scrupulous attention to detail. As a warrior you need to find the true fighters on your team who will have the guts to make difficult decisions on its behalf. As the king/queen you need to have both diversity and compassion on your team to ensure that all the members are complementing one another without overriding individual goals or ambitions. As the magician, you need to create opportunities that people will rise to achieve without letting them think that you've had anything to do with it. And as the lover, you need to pay attention to every single detail of your team so that the right decisions are made, the highest productivity is reached, and the stage is set to raise the bar on the possibilities for the next round of growth and prosperity. Find your unique leadership profile—and recognize that pulling it all together is as much a function of working through the first four team dysfunctions as it is to paying attention to the details while keeping your eye on the big picture at all times.

> **What's most important about the concept of belonging and creating core communities in the ambitious journey is the ongoing commitment to creating a place that's enticing, engaging, and motivating for others to want to belong to.**

A FINAL WORD

Belonging is an all-encompassing concept that's hard to cover in one short chapter. I strongly encourage you to follow up this notion of belonging by reading material that relates to your particular area directly, whether it be branding (personal or product), creating a viable corporate culture, attracting talent and customers, rebuilding your career aspirations, or refocusing your commitment to the work you currently do. What's most important about the concept of belonging and creating core communities in the ambitious journey is the ongoing commitment to creating a place that's enticing, engaging, and motivating for others to want to belong to. For those who want to maintain influence, it will open doors and smooth the way for future success. For leaders and managers, it will leverage your human capital far beyond what you directly contribute or those you oversee. That is the power of creating belonging that lasts.

While looking for a way to bring the concept of belonging full circle and laying the groundwork for the next rule of ambition, momentum, I found myself going back to a fascinating interview I did in February 2003, in the midst of one of New York City's worst snowstorms. I walked off Fifth Avenue and made my way up into the opulent, old-world apartment of Eleanor Lambert Berkson. Her assistant led me into a room replete with beautiful, precious antiques, where I was graciously welcomed by a well-dressed, very poised woman. Within an hour, Eleanor had revealed fascinating stories of the hundred years of her life. She reeled off names, places, and dates with ease while I scribbled away, barely able to keep up.

Eleanor is best known as the publicist who established the international stature of American fashion. She helped to create the Costume Institute at the Metropolitan Museum of Art, the Coty Awards, and the Council of Fashion Designers of America. In 1941 Eleanor established the International Best Dressed Poll, which showcased such top New York designers as Bill Blass and Oscar de la Renta and which continued under her aegis until her death in October 2003, just months after I interviewed her.

She is a prime example of someone who knew how to create belonging in every sense of the word. For each of her undertakings she called every fashion journalist from around the world and pitched her concept. She intuitively elicited in them a desire to belong to something that was participatory and that was based on pride in ownership; she played the pluralist in her ability to appeal to each and every one of her contacts in a meaningful way; and she certainly was the ultimate catalyst for change by creating a new institution within the fashion industry.

Eleanor used the leadership qualities of the warrior, queen, lover, and magician to pull it all together so that participants, press, and the general public wanted to identify with her fashion sense and her fashion events long after they became the center of her own world. That's the sign of a true ambitionist, who not only knows how to create belonging in the moment but understands that she's building the key ingredient in the next rule for ambitionists: building momentum that has lasting effect.

RULE 4
MOMENTUM

> Ambition can creep as well as soar.
> —*Edmund Burke*

Serious cyclists always hit a point in the race when they face a wall, and only by recommitting to their determination are they able to get past this physical and mental barrier. It's called the "second discipline." Once they get past that moment they enter what is, in effect, the second phase of their race—and they often gain confidence knowing that they've got the stamina to finish and quite possibly to win.

Whether you're a cyclist set on winning a race or a careerist focused on building success, it's the management of momentum that will allow you to both capitalize on the speed and energy you've already put in place and overcome any unexpected barriers along the way. By way of example, I turn to the well-known celebrity and advertising photographer EJ Camp.

EJ has shot many covers for *Rolling Stone* magazine and photographed the hottest movie stars around. She's known for finding a way to bring out the best in her subjects. When I interviewed EJ, between her cross-country stints from New York to Hollywood, she was very concise about her understanding of momentum: "Your career is either growing or shrinking. There really is no in between. So the only way to use momentum to your advantage is to keep building while you're on the upward curve, find ways to keep up your stamina when the pressure is on, and always plan for ways to reignite your momentum when times are tough. In this business, it's essential. Many photographers mistake being busy for being challenged, and that gives you a false sense of security. No matter how many back-to-back photo shoots I have, I always ensure that I'm creating a new photo mailer to send out to clients and agents alike that will capture my newest work. You always have to be pushing yourself and building your portfolio and thinking about what's next. I suspect it's no different in other industries."

EJ, like other ambitionists, knows that momentum is easier to build upon when you're revved up at a certain speed. But she's been in the business long enough to know that no matter how successful you are, there's always an unexpected dip or a disastrous, unforeseen event that can cripple your momentum-building efforts and potentially change the course of your "race." She experienced her own worst standstill in a most dramatic way.

"September 11 totally set me back. I was working for Pepsi that day and we were in the tallest building besides the World Trade Center—the Helmsley Building. We were setting up lighting before the photo shoot. Looking out the floor-to-ceiling windows as we drank our coffee, we saw the World Trade Center on fire. At first none of us really understood what was happening—it was almost like a dream in slow motion. But when the second plane hit, the reality of the situation was overwhelming, and we were all in a state of shock. The anguish we all felt at that moment as we contemplated the impact that event would have on the people in that building was life changing. It was devastating. I equate that moment with when everything stopped with my career for a long time. Companies pulled back, celebrities kept a low profile—all of us were hit. Aside from the personal impact, I realized that managing momentum was always something I had relied on as part of the natural ebb and flow of my career. Suddenly I was faced with a complete stop in time. All of us had to pull together, and with a renewed sense of what *really* matters to begin to slowly build up momentum in our lives and our work once again."

BUILDING LONGEVITY EN ROUTE

Rule 4 marks the second half of the ambition cycle. Once you've made the journey of discovery (Rule 1), honed your focus and decision-making skills (Rule 2), and created your core communities through belonging (Rule 3), you need to learn the art of momentum—how to extend your ambition over the long term and build on your own renewable resources. Learning to manage momentum will help you regroup and find your second discipline.

Canadian-born Hilary Brown, a foreign correspondent with ABC, puts it this way: "I'd describe momentum as being on a roll, which means that the more you succeed, the more you succeed, and nothing succeeds . . . like success. But this never lasts . . . most careers have highs and lows, and the lows aren't always your fault." Every journey indeed has its ebbs and flows, and there will be times when things seem slow, bogged down, even moving backward. The trick is to find a way to ignite the second discipline during these inevitable lag times. And for ambitionists, this means first developing the right mindset to approach momentum effectively.

I found the starting point for describing momentum when I interviewed the Canadian interior design duo behind the world-acclaimed firm Yabu Pushelberg. From the design of the W Times Square hotel in New York City to the redesign of Tiffany & Co.'s Fifth Avenue flagship store and the Four Seasons Hotel in Marunouchi, Tokyo, Yabu Pushelberg has built up a wave of interior design that has caught the attention of the world. As one journalist put it, "If doing what you love for a living is the measure for success, then Glenn Pushelberg and George Yabu are arguably two of the most successful interior designers in the world." What's more, they show no signs of slowing down.

> "Momentum? Well, let's see . . . I think it's this visual concept of a kind of internal gyroscope. Some days you whip that cord and drive yourself and achieve what you want with resourcefulness and force . . . and other days you can't even *find* the rip cord."

When I asked them to describe momentum building in the context of their careers, George responded with an interesting image. "Momentum? Well, let's see . . . I think it's this visual concept of a kind of internal gyroscope. Some days you whip that cord and drive yourself and achieve what you want with resourcefulness and force . . . and other days you can't even *find* the rip cord. You know it's there, but you don't have the energy to rev up the internal engines. What keeps the internal gyroscope moving is the knowledge that momentum is a resource that you have to take care of, nurture, and build up. In return it'll provide you with your next phase of ambition. If we think about what we want to do next, we always say we don't want more but we want better, more interesting—we want to redefine that internal gyroscope and build on the momentum we've carefully built."

This metaphor of an internal gyroscope makes sense if you think of it as a spinning top. In aircrafts it's arguably the most important instrument: no matter what angle the plane is flying at, it shows the pilot where straight and level is. The image of the gyroscope reminds us that we ourselves are responsible for our speed and pace at any time during our journey. Yabu Pushelberg manage momentum in their business so that it not only generates success, but the kind of success that interests them—self-directed progress. And momentum naturally progresses from the belonging stage of the ambition cycle; that is, after building up others' desire to identify with your cause comes a refocus on self.

Here's a quick overview of the three strategies required for momentum:

Developing momentum This first stage requires the most diverse set of skills and tactics, and in some ways is the most important of the three. The focus here is on proactively putting the wheels in motion to generate energy and drive. After all, it's only when you have all the pieces in place that you can realistically assess the opportunities that come your way, anticipate your opponents' moves, and find ways to leverage your skills. And while ambitionists push the envelope on their momentum, they "work their trade" by continuing to do what they're best at and by telling and retelling the story of how they evolved to the level of success they've achieved thus far. In a way, this is the setup for the ensuing strategies.

Sustaining momentum Once you reach a certain degree of success, the focus shifts toward finding ways to carefully monitor and focus your energy. To do this, ambitionists learn to play the role of the editor. That means keeping a certain distance from your own success—and at the same time having the insight to jump on opportunities that will propel you ahead of the curve. The role of the editor translates into "less is more."

Reigniting momentum At one point or another, people find themselves facing a lack of momentum. Because this often happens without warning, you'll need to prepare for the inevitable ebbs in the flow by re-creating your passion, retelling the story of who you are and what differentiates you in the marketplace, and even finding ways to redefine momentum itself.

Let's look at these strategies in more detail.

Developing Momentum

Beginnings are always exciting, and it's no different for building momentum. Everyone I interviewed spoke fondly about the energy and thrill of developing momentum in their lifework.

READY YOURSELF

Jerry Mitchell is a top Broadway choreographer whose hits include *Hairspray, The Full Monty, The Rocky Horror Show,* and *Gypsy Rose,* as well as several films, including *Scent of a Woman* and *In and Out.* He's also someone who has built his career on readiness.

Born in the small town of Paw Paw, Michigan, Jerry was always fascinated with dance. At the age of five he would watch his neighbor take dance classes and then help her practice at home, and at eight he got involved in a local theater group called the Paw Paw Village Players and joined the chorus of *The Music Man*. "I guess it was at that point," he says, "that I caught the dance bug. I remember telling my mother that I was going to one day dance on Broadway and nothing was going to get in my way."

In his senior year at high school, Jerry went to a local shopping mall to see a production of *West Side Story* by a troupe called the Young Americans. One of the dancers, as it turned out, had been hurt. "I followed the group back to the auditorium and kept dancing around the lobby, trying to catch the attention of the director. I did, and he invited me to join the troupe for the year. I knew it would require missing school, but I also knew I was ready to experience dancing full time. My readiness was in full swing."

By the time he was twenty-three, Jerry was dancing in his fifth Broadway show. For some that would be enough. But for Jerry, readying himself always meant branching out and trying new things. When he was asked to choreograph his first equity production of *The Amazing Technicolor Dream Coat* while still dancing for a Broadway production, he worked out an arrangement with the director whereby he would take a few weeks off to do the choreography. In exchange, he agreed to stay on with the show an extra six months. Generally unheard of on Broadway, this was yet another example of how Jerry knew when to take advantage of his own readiness.

His career continued to leapfrog from dance to choreography, from live

"If momentum is a renewable resource, which I think it is, then what you're trying to get to is the inner kernel of what drove you there in the first place, and to stay in contact with what you're really prepared to take on."

theater to film, from off Broadway to Broadway. "If momentum is a renewable resource, which I think it is, then what you're trying to get to is the inner kernel of what drove you there in the first place, and to stay in contact with what you're really prepared to take on. You're the only person who can say when you're ready to move on, to up the ante. It's almost as if you need to catch yourself in the midst of a dialogue with yourself, and ready yourself to keep moving on."

KNOW WHERE YOU ARE IN THE GAME

Mackie Shilstone is what's known as a performance enhancement expert at the Ochsner Clinic Foundation in New Orleans. He is perhaps most famous for his work as a performance enhancement expert with Michael Spinks, a former world lightweight champion who with Mackie's help became the world heavyweight champion—a first in the history of boxing. Seventeen years later Mackie applied this same model of performance management with Roy Jones Jr., and succeeded once again. His work with Hall of Fame shortstop Ozzie Smith of the St. Louis Cardinals, and as many as twenty-five hundred other professional athletes, has put him on the map as a top-notch performance manager as well as the best-selling author of *Maximum Energy for Life*. Let's look at a few of his guiding principles, beginning with knowing where you are in the game at all times.

Mackie starts out working with athletes by defining where they are: how far along they are in their career, the state of their physical and mental health, and what their goals are moving forward. It's an approach he'd recommend to the everyday individual as well. "I challenge everyone to know where they stand in terms of their health, their stamina, and their overall makeup to determine how much they are physically, mentally and spiritually able to take on." Mackie points to the fact that the majority of people who have heart attacks today have no warning symptoms. "They've never taken stock of their health and what level they wanted to play the game of life. And by the time they have a heart attack, it's too late."

Recognizing where you are in your game translates into taking stock of what you've built up in your portfolio of skills, in your ability to focus and make decisions, and in your ability as a leader to realistically assess both your weaknesses and strengths. In doing this on a regular basis, you'll be able to assess how much stamina you have to maintain your level of excellence, speed, and success. And by knowing what level of play you're capable of, you can plan your course of action ahead of time, before you enter the ring.

Knowing where you are in the game also involves a sense of anticipation. Mackie says he's never met a boxer who describes himself as being in the business of "taking a punch." Rather, they're in the business of knowing where the next punch is going to come from and anticipating it. Likewise for ambitionists, who control their momentum so that they're prepared for what it may bring their way. Just as EJ Camp talked about building momentum when she's busiest—in anticipation of slower times—ambitionists cum boxers anticipate how decisions will affect them and are prepared for the next punch.

In Rule 3, belonging, we talked about the importance of recognizing that besides the group goal, all team members have their own personal ambitions. In momentum, however, it's the ambitions of your *opponents* that become the focus. Your opponents may be your individual competitors, but they may also take the form of time, money, or market conditions. However you define them, the key is to identify them and know what they're all about.

Mackie tells a story that encapsulates this concept: "When I was working with Roy Jones Jr. and was challenged with moving him from a lightweight championship to a heavyweight championship, I applied this exact strategy: I assessed our opponent, John Ruiz, who at this point had close to forty-three wins. I also knew that he was the first Latin American heavyweight champion, and that when he won the WBA title from Evander Holyfield it took him six hours to wend his way through the crowds from the airport to his home in San Juan, Puerto Rico, normally a two-hour drive, and then address a stadium filled with over thirty thousand fans. This spoke volumes. I realized that we had a very nationalistic man who was very proud, someone who was fighting for something. So, we had to have a strategic plan that would compromise his pride. If we did this, he'd pay more attention to his pride than his opponent—who was my guy, Roy Jones Jr.

"In my mind, it doesn't matter if we're talking about a boxer, a marketing strategy, or a career move—it's really all about anticipating where you have to be to keep your momentum strategic at all times."

"As part of my research I knew that of his forty-three wins, 60 percent came in his first few rounds, 20 percent came in the last few rounds, and all his losses came in round twelve. I came to the conclusion that he recovered in round seven and round nine. Knowing this, we chose to go on the attack in rounds seven and nine—anticipating his recovery periods. By having a plan like that, we built up Roy Jones Jr.'s momentum to meet the weaknesses of this opponent. In my mind, it doesn't matter if we're talking about a boxer, a marketing strategy, or a career move—it's really all about anticipating where you have to be to keep your momentum strategic at all times."

ACCUMULATE YOUR PERSONAL BARGAINING CHIPS

With these sports guidelines in hand, ambitionists are now ready to build momentum by leveraging their talent. In Rule 3 we talked about how important it is to connect with leveragers: those people who can help put your skills or product out into the world. In momentum terms, leverage is what provides you with the power to move from one position or one job to another. Rather than simply accruing a list of individual credentials that, while valuable on their own, don't build one upon one another, leveraging your portfolio of skills creates a wake of momentum behind and around you that builds on itself. To illustrate the point, I turn again to the Hollywood photographer EJ Camp.

When EJ graduated from Rochester Institute of Technology she assessed her talents and recognized that aside from artistic ability, she had good people skills. Given this knowledge (knowing where she stood in her game), she took a chance and switched from a major in art to a photography major, which led her directly to the world of fashion photography. In other words, she called in her first bargaining chip and chose to leverage her artistic ability and people skills by redirecting her college degree to suit her talents and her lifestyle goals.

EJ ended up getting a job with renowned photographers Albert Watson and Bruce Webber, working as their assistant for several years. The job was trying but exciting—she learned how to deal with all kinds of personalities while traveling the world and coping with extreme pressure. But after living in Milan for a year she returned to the US, tired of what she called "the teenage runaway set." What she needed, she realized, was to move out of fashion photography altogether.

Instead of simply finding another way to use her talents in fashion photography, EJ focused on the skills she had accumulated—her ability to work with fashion models, to manage tight deadlines, and to cope with lots of travel—and pitched her work to the publishers of *Rolling Stone*. It worked. Her first cover for the magazine, featuring Christie Brinkley, was an instant success. This opened the door, and she began focusing her energy on the world of rock and roll. But, although the lifestyle was fast and exciting, after a few years she wanted to turn up the volume once again—not more but better, different. Yes, she was busy, but why not translate her success into something new?

Around this time EJ was asked to shoot Tom Cruise for a *Rolling Stone* cover. As it turned out, she and Cruise come from the same hometown, and they hit it off. Cruise asked her to do the movie poster photography for his films *Top Gun* and *The Color of Money*, and before she knew it she had stridden right into the Hollywood celebrity venue.

At every transition, EJ used the same strategy to effectively build momentum: she leveraged her accumulated talents and skills, repackaged them, and called in her bargaining chips as a means of moving on to her next big success.

WORK YOUR TRADE

Practicality is always part of the ambitionist's plan. In the discovery stage we talked about the importance of leaning into your discovery and finding ways to work around what you think you might want to do. Similarly, in the momentum stage, it's important to keep "working your trade" while you build and anticipate your next important move.

According to the July 2003 issue of *Restaurant Hospitality*, "There may be no hotter restaurant operator in the country today than Stephen Starr." As he's a restaurateur of well-known establishments such as the Continental, Morimoto, and Buddakan (the latter voted one of America's top fifty restaurants in *Travel & Leisure* magazine), it's little wonder that I turn to Stephen for insights into how to build momentum by working his trade.

"When I was sixteen I wanted to be a television producer, a filmmaker, *and* a DJ—I wanted all those careers. I think this desire to produce and create has never left me." Not one to wonder idly about the possibilities, Stephen rolled up his sleeves, studied each of those trades, and began to test his abilities. Along the way, his experiences were educational and entertaining to boot. At sixteen, for example, he and a friend filmed a Todd Rundgren concert and wanted to pitch it to NBC for its *In Concert* program. But he figured that if he was going to work in TV he had to start at the top. And sure enough, Stephen managed to make an appointment with the brass: "I still remember walking toward the meeting with my dad's briefcase, and all I had in it were socks and underwear for my overnight trip. I almost didn't care if they bought the video, I just knew that I was going to meet the president of NBC." On another occasion, Stephen pitched Viacom a cooking show with Yulles Gibbons as the host. "Viacom was very keen on Yulles and we were so close to closing the deal. Then old Yulles died on us, and that was the end of that one!"

Stephen took this same tenacity and sense of humor with him throughout his career. After he'd tried radio production and working as a DJ, his keen interest in production and drama led him into the nightclub business. Soon he was running one of the top comedy nightclubs in Philadelphia, showcasing the likes of

Sandra Bernhard and Jerry Seinfeld. He went on to build a top rock concert promotion business, handling such megastars as Madonna and U2. And all of this before he leveraged his accumulated skills in negotiation, entertainment, and design to the restaurant business!

"If I look back on it, I worked my trade—whether it was in the music business, concert business, nightclub business, and even today, in the restaurant business. I apply gusto and I pay attention to the details. When I first started out in the nightclub business, I did everything from writing the ads, to booking the comedians, to negotiating every detail of the contracts. This same attention to detail is still at the heart of what I do today. Ultimately, I embrace the trade I'm in. And so far it's worked well."

> **Working your trade isn't just about how much time and energy you put into it, but rather how targeted you are in the process. And that requires a healthy dose of research and preparation.**

Working your trade isn't just about how much time and energy you put into it, but rather how targeted you are in the process. And that requires a healthy dose of research and preparation to ensure that all your efforts are strategically sound and will produce the best results possible. We already know how much research and preparation Mackie Shilstone does on behalf of his clients to help them prepare for a match in the boxing ring. This same dedication is crucial to all the high-profile people I interviewed in this category. The bottom line—there's no substitute for being prepared and no shortcut to the research that needs to be done. Just as we talked about the importance of paying attention to detail as a means of pulling a team together in Rule 3, the same attention to detail holds true for the momentum stage.

Stephen knew nothing about the food business before he ran his restaurants, but he learned the ropes and hired the experts to ensure the operations run smoothly. And he still commits to preparing himself every day. "To me, staying close to the customer is crucial in the restaurant business. I only once ignored this important lesson and the restaurant, though on the road to success, went under because the food didn't work. Today, I never ask the waiters and chefs how many steaks were sold. Who cares! What I want to know is *why* clients liked the steaks. What was best about them? In taking the time to ask these questions, I'm already forming in my mind the new menu for these very same customers."

EJ Camp works her trade with the same level of preparedness: "You can go into the studio and have a great concept in your head for a particular celebrity, and they can shoot it down right out of the gate. If you're not prepared with a concept that you're pretty sure they're going to be comfortable with, you can lose your cool, you can choke creatively—and believe me, the shoot will not be a success. I always have a few ideas going in, and in some ways I let the actor tell me what he or she is most comfortable with. That to me is a sign of someone who's done their research and has a true grasp of their craft.

"I remember the day I shot Tom Cruise for the *Top Gun* movie poster. He arrived on set way before the call and before Kelly McGillis arrived. He had a side conversation with me in which he gently explained that Kelly, who is very tall, was really sensitive about her height, so he asked me to pay careful attention to the height difference between them. Of course, when she arrived she was wearing really high heels, and I realized that it was Tom's way of ensuring that he had anticipated and prepared for all elements of the photo shoot—including his accommodation of height differences! He took the time and energy to arrive early and effectively position the situation in a way that made everyone look good in the end. And right down to the last details—he always follows up every photo shoot with a thank-you card and a small gift. I admire that kind of attention to detail. That sense of preparation."

DO WHAT YOU DO BEST

Many ambitionists, myself included, are attracted to what's new, to ideas of change, and to what's different. That's important in the discovery stage and helpful in overcoming risk aversion during important decision-making times. But when you're building your momentum, it's sometimes best to simply do what you're best at.

Mackie Shilstone talks about how athletes always need to remember what got them into the big league in the first place. "Ozzie Smith went to the hall of fame because he was the best shortstop ever. At the age of thirty, he only wanted three more years, but I helped him get eleven years. The truth is, when he first came to me, he said he wanted to be known as a better hitter. I asked him, 'What signed your contract?' Of course, it was his defenseman skills. So I said, 'What if I made you a better hitter but you lost your defenseman skills?' Needless to say, we focused on increasing his batting average, and he won the golden glove every year thereafter—but he was still known as the one with the best defenseman skills."

EMBRACE STORYTELLING AND MYTH

For individuals and companies alike, storytelling and myth making are almost magical ingredients in the building of momentum. A recent *Fast Company* article attests to the power of word of mouth:

"What is the sound of a nation questioning the meaning of success and the value of money? According to Ed Keller and John Berry, CEO and senior research director, respectively, of Roper ASW, it's the sound of peer-to-peer conversation rather than Madison Avenue pitches or Wall Street formulas. More and more, these world-class opinion analysts argue, the opinions that matter most are those that flow person to person—whether it's over the back fence or across the internet."

In his book *The Tipping Point: How Little Things Can Make a Big Difference,* Malcolm Gladwell talks, among other things, about the importance of rumors and what he refers to as the "stickiness" of a product or service. He cites as an example the rebirth of Hush Puppy shoes. In 1994–95, Wolverine, which makes Hush Puppies, was about to phase out the shoes that originally made it famous. But then came a strange turn of events—Hush Puppies were suddenly becoming hip among Manhattan club and bar-goers. Such influential designers as Isaac Mizrahi and Anna Sui began to request them, which of course only further enhanced the allure of these humble shoes. In 1995 Wolverine had sold 430,000 pairs of the classic Hush Puppies. The next year it sold four times as many, and the year after that still more. And *that*, as Gladwell points out, is storytelling in motion.

The Blair Witch Project, the famously low-budget horror film, is another great example of how myth making and storytelling can build momentum. Created by three students, this independent film generated more buzz than almost any other horror film ever made. Before it even opened it had inspired over twenty fan sites, a mailing list, a Web ring, a Usenet group, and more than its fair share of glowing reports on the influential movie site Ain't It Cool News. Its makers focused on internet marketing, engaging friends and associates to generate fan sites and word of mouth in an organized fashion. The question of whether they used deceptive cyberspace marketing as a means of generating false reviews continues to be debated, but it's clear that *The Blair Witch Project* was one of the first in cross-media storytelling.

When it comes to storytelling in the world of nutrition and sports enhancement, there's nothing like word of mouth and athletic endorsement. But for new kids on the block, these endorsements aren't always easy to get. G-Push, a small, UK-based specialist sports drink company that entered the marketplace in January 2000, is a good case in point. Having developed products based on a novel carbohydrate, galactose, which tests had shown to enhance and sustain energy for athletes, they went about building up their reputation specifically through the first-hand accounts of athletes who used these products for specific races and competitions.

When Chris McCormack, one of the world's leading triathletes, didn't finish his highly anticipated 2002 Hawaii Ironman Race, he cited nutrition as one of his issues and set about correcting it for 2003. As noted on the G-Push website, here's what McCormack communicates to other athletes: "What can I say about G-Push that I haven't already said. This is the only fluid replacement solution that I will ever use. . . . I have packed and taken my own G-Push on the course now at all my races. The results speak for themselves. I mean it

> **Word of mouth is what can move a product, company, or individual into high-gear momentum at crucial stages of growth. In the end, it's often the story that lingers and the myth that entices people.**

when I say, if you're not using G-Push and your competitors are, we really do have an unfair advantage."

A simple endorsement of this kind, aimed at such a highly targeted audience as amateur and professional athletes and competing against giants with unlimited resources, can be just the key to trigger confidence in a new product—and serves as a testament to the power of storytelling.

Word of mouth is what can move a product, company, or individual into high-gear momentum at crucial stages of growth. In the end, it's often the story that lingers and the myth that entices people. The casual but highly coveted conversations cited in *Fast Company* above provide invaluable product marketing, and those who leverage these tools will go a long way toward building momentum for their product, service, or career.

There's a natural progression of tactics in building momentum. Ambitionists begin by readying themselves psychologically to take advantage of opportunities as they come their way. They then focus on the game at hand, anticipating opponents' moves as part of understanding that game. When it's time to make a move into something untried, they call in their chips and leverage their talents as a means of progressing from one opportunity to another. Ambitionists offset any risk incurred by continuing to work their trade, paying attention to the details as a means of being the best at what they do. And by incorporating storytelling, they remind themselves and others of who they are and what they've built to date—another means of adding the power of history and track record to their momentum. With these tactics in place, ambitionists are now ready to move to the second stage of momentum.

Sustaining Momentum

The movement from building to maintaining momentum parallels the earlier transition from discovery to focus; that is, a relatively free-form openness is followed by a more focused, rigorous process. That's because the pacing required in maintaining momentum entails a certain amount of whittling down and editing. Let's look at the specifics.

LEARN TO EDIT

When George Yabu and Glenn Pushelberg started out in the design business, they would take on anything they were offered. "We were hungry to do design work—a photocopy shop, a shoe chain, whatever. And we were able to not only survive but do well enough to support the one or two small, high-end design projects that we loved to do but that didn't generate any revenue for us.

"We always had a certain curiosity and fear of boredom. And in the end, it was exactly this curiosity and fear that forced us to re-evaluate the momentum we were building—to stop for long enough to determine that we needed to change the direction of the work we were doing or we'd forever remain in the world of mediocrity. And that was not where our true ambition lay."

George and Glenn slowly phased out those clients who were no longer suited to their ultimate ambition of high-end design. They focused on those who would parlay their talent into specific projects that would let them play the role of "design sociologists"—to appeal to emotions and usage rather than design fads. Glenn explains: "We're good editors of our own work. We edit out all the excess design. This translates into longevity of space usage for our clients—in other words, our designs will last longer than their property lease!—and also gives us longevity in our own momentum."

As reflected in Yabu Pushelberg's strategy, then, the editor's role applies not only to the clients you surround yourself with but also to the projects themselves. In a sense, you need to develop a conveyor belt of ideas and make sure that the caliber of clients you attract and the opportunities you choose match those ideas. Rather than building unbridled momentum, you'll maintain a discerning and sustainable focus.

Jerry Mitchell's interpretation of the editor's role is reflected in the collaborative projects he takes on. While his career was skyrocketing, he suffered many personal losses—friends who died of AIDS. Over the years he's spent countless hours doing volunteer work for Broadway Cares and Broadway Equity Fights AIDS in their efforts to raise money. While he was working on the *Will Rogers Follies* show, someone suggested that he choreograph a dance act to raise money for Broadway Cares. So, in the spirit of helping others, he and five other dancers performed an act he had choreographed, raising $8,000 in one night. Based on that smashing success Jerry added women to the show, and the eighteen-member troupe went on to raise $18,000 dollars. Broadway Cares eventually became one of the show's producers and in 2002, twelve years after the initial event, they raised $400,000 in one night thanks to the contribution of people like Jerry and the 185 dancers on stage.

"What it allowed me to do as a choreographer was work with the top dancers in New York for a benefit that was extremely important. At the same time, it gave me a chance to choreograph for free, which in turn got my name out there, and perhaps in your terms, is an example of me 'working my trade.' And in fact it led to my being asked to choreograph *The Full Monty*, which led to *Rocky Horror Show*, and on and on. But what stuck with me was the notion of collaboration. The momentum I was able to maintain wasn't because I did it all myself. I learned how to collaborate and work with others as a means of ensuring that the quality of the show would never be jeopardized because I was too busy at my day job. Today, my volunteer work involves collaboration with a whole team of choreographers. When I was younger I tried to do everything by myself. As a more mature 'ambitionist'—as you would say—I've learned the importance of pacing myself so as to maintain momentum through the power and joy that come with collaboration."

STAY JUST AHEAD OF THE CURVE

Finding ways to proactively counteract competition without expending too much energy is crucial to sustaining momentum. That's because regardless of what industry you're in, it gives you just enough information and knowledge to stay ahead of the curve. For many people who work in creative fields, the most challenging competition comes from those who play copycat, providing look-alike products and services for a fraction of the price. Whether it's the fabric that Tricia Guild designs, the products that Karim Rashid creates, or the spaces that Yabu Pushelberg dream up, there are always competitors who try to mimic excellence and play the price game with unsuspecting customers.

This same hurdle crops up for anyone in an industry that relies on interpretation and creativity, whether it be in marketing and advertising, television and film production, or consulting of any kind. In these industries, there's always some novice competitor who claims to be able to produce the same thing for less. Only well-informed customers can differentiate between the quality of one product and service versus that of another. Those ambitionists who take the time to educate their clients in how to discern quality will stay ahead of the price curve by eliminating a price comparison as the qualifier for buying. And in the process, they can often solidify their working relationships with clients as a reliable information source to turn to in a confusing, fast-paced industry.

One of the best ways to counteract this potential barrier is to surprise and delight customers—and disarm competitors—by narrowing your focus even further without any warning. Yabu Pushelberg stay ahead of the design curve by constantly evolving their focus and surprising the marketplace. Based on the industry recognition and acclaim for work they did with Tiffany & Co. and Bergdorf Goodman, everyone assumed that they were going to brand themselves as retail designers. But instead they parlayed their expertise into designing hotels and resorts, adding such clients as Starwood Hotels & Resorts. These projects naturally led them to other hotel work, from designing the flagship W hotels in New York to collaborations with Four Seasons Hotels and Resorts, Hyatt International, and MGM, to name a few. Peers and associates immediately assumed they had switched their focus to hotels. But again they plan to stay ahead of the curve by refocusing and repositioning their expertise.

"Even though we like to work with these hotels, we don't want to *only* be known as the W hotel guys," explains Glenn. "And so it's important for us to protect our brand through our next strategic focus. Our goal is to design gems around the world. How we define that is what keeps us fresh, new, and surprising."

KEEP JUST ENOUGH DISTANCE

To "be on a roll," as Hilary Brown describes it, implies a certain amount of energy and speed that's somewhat beyond our control. It's difficult to take a pause; it would be like gazing up at the clouds while riding a wave on a surfboard—you'd likely lose both your balance and your momentum. But once ambitionists enter the maintenance stage, it's the ability to *avoid* getting caught up in your own momentum that will allow you to make sound decisions. Just as ambitionists must think like a trader in Rule 2—and know when to walk away from a deal that will inevitably go south—they must also know when to apply just enough distance to pace themselves accordingly when sustaining momentum.

One of the best ways to look at establishing this stance is through a concept known as "performance management." Today, if you scan the business section in bookstores, you're sure to come across a host of new books that focus on managing one's performance and its relationship to the working world. The key here is to vary both the speed with which you perform and the length of the recovery periods you need to recuperate sufficiently. Whether you're a professional athlete pacing yourself for your next series or a salesperson looking for ways to extend your momentum over the next four quarters in a tough market, it's your ability to manage your performance and distance yourself from the moment that can make the difference.

Mackie Shilstone has a helpful rule: "Play like a rookie, but act like a veteran." Here's how he describes it: "The rookie goes all out at practice and gives it his best. When the practice is over, he has to go home and recuperate so that he has the stamina to get back on the field the next day again. The veteran goes on the field and focuses all his energy on doing what he does best. When practice is over he plays nine holes of golf with his buddies and knows he'll have the necessary stamina to get on the field and do a top-notch job the next day. The rookie has a tremendous amount of energy but has limited experience in knowing how to move efficiently from point A to point B. The veteran, on the other hand, knows how to get from point A to point B with the smallest possible expenditure of energy. And that makes all the difference."

> **Keeping just enough distance doesn't mean you're indifferent to your career, company, or idea; rather, it's what allows you to pace yourself with confidence.**

Stephen Starr committed the enthusiasm of a rookie to each trade he worked. Ultimately, though, he was a veteran who hired the experts, put the pieces in place, and did only what he was best at. EJ similarly didn't expend energy on art when she knew photography would better suit her, nor did she blindly continue in fashion photography when she was ready to move into something else. In short, she played the veteran at each transition by pacing herself along the way.

Keeping just enough distance doesn't mean you're indifferent to your career, company, or idea; rather, it's what allows you to pace yourself with confidence. Those in the business world often look for exactly this skill as a mark of success. Potential investors looking at startup companies, for example, can be just as interested in how the company leaders deal with the negotiation process as they are in the business plans they draw up and the presentations they make.

These investors have been known to throw a few wrenches into the works just to see how the CEO and the executive team handle surprise and uncertainty when the heat's on. And if that startup's leaders have learned the art of detachment, they'll be able to slightly remove themselves from the moment—just enough to maintain perspective on the negotiations. In other words, they consciously maintain enough momentum to keep the investment deal in play without expending unnecessary energy that might be interpreted as overeagerness.

A real estate developer relates this story: "At one point we had bought and built two or three restaurant properties for a high-profile investor that became extremely successful. When he approached us to develop his fourth property, I had to stay removed enough from the situation to determine if my company should commit to another project with this same investor. Although we enjoyed working with him, in the end we turned it down because we wanted to widen our developer portfolio in anticipation of more international growth that we were planning for. Yes, we could have had another hugely successful project on our hands in the short run, but by maintaining what you call 'a certain amount of distance' we were able to stand back and make the best strategic decision for us long term."

Reigniting Momentum

Robert Cushing said, "If I advance, follow me. If I stop, push me. If I fall, inspire me." These words form the basis for the third strategy. Whether you're experiencing a lull in sales, a lack of response to your résumé in your job search efforts, or an unexplained silence from your most reliable clients, at one point or other we all hit a plateau. Let's look at what ambitionists do to jump-start the process when this happens.

BUILD ON THE OUTTAKES

When EJ Camp found herself overwhelmed by 9/11, she needed something to help inspire her. Interestingly, rather than turn to her best work to buoy her spirits, she decided to re-examine her outtake photographs from over the years. "By forcing myself to look at what I'd put aside, what clients rejected in my photographs, I was able to find patterns, see trends, and discover the beginnings of new ideas that weren't fully developed yet, that weren't successfully implemented, but that represented the kernels of inspiration that would take me to the next level of my own career. It took a lot of hard work, but it propelled me forward." Based on these outtakes, EJ ended up generating a whole new promotional campaign.

Keeping a folder of your "outtakes"—the projects, concepts, proposals, and ideas that weren't accepted at the time—is an excellent way to reignite your momentum. You just may discover a new way to package your talents or a means for initiating your next move.

CREATE TRACTION

Momentum is about energy and movement. We all know that it's a lot easier to go from fifty to a hundred miles an hour than it is to go from a dead standstill to the hundred-mile mark. Sometimes it's outside influences—a downturn in the market, a world crisis—that force you to a standstill. But at other times it's you who can become your worst enemy. A sense of complacency may take over, and before you know it you're in a hiatus. One of the best ways to stay on your toes is to consciously introduce a little conflict or friction into the scenario. Ambitionists call this "creating traction."

Stephen Starr, for example, constantly applied traction to his game plan. From his first big hit, the Rat Pack–themed Continental

Restaurant, to the Buddakan Restaurant with its chic decor and modern Asian cuisine, Stephen has always recognized the need to create just enough tension between the elements. In each case, he deciphered what people defined as fun, sophisticated, or comforting and then built a whole restaurant aesthetic around it. By doing so, he's been able to continually capture the attention of his demographic.

When an ambitionist detects a lull, the conscious introduction of a sense of tension is simply a means to establish a new platform. This will instantly put you back into the driver's seat, back into a state of proactively building momentum. And the momentum cycle is ready to begin again.

A FINAL WORD

Of all the rules for ambition, Rule 4 is perhaps most indicative of the fact that this journey requires constant management and design. By applying specific tactics to the building, maintaining, and reigniting of momentum, ambitionists learn how to handle success by controlling its specific speed and velocity. The careful strategies applied here will determine which ambitionists can succeed not just once, but many times over, each time taking the learning with them as they move forward.

When an ambitionist detects a lull, the conscious introduction of a sense of tension is simply a means to establish a new platform. This will instantly put you back into the driver's seat.

When I interviewed Jerry Mitchell at the Duke rehearsal studios on New York's Forty-second Street, he was rehearsing for Sam

Mendes's *Gypsy Rose*. As actresses, assistant choreographers, and musicians filed into the rehearsal studio I asked him my last question: "How would you describe your journey to date?" Just at that moment, the stage manager asked if he was ready to start afternoon rehearsals. He replied, "Yup, I'm on my way." Then he turned to me and said, "Ditto—in answer to your question."

That pretty well summed up momentum for me. To the outside eye, Jerry has "made it," if you will. But for him the ride is continuous motion. He's simply gathering momentum for the next leg of his ambitious journey.

RULE 5
BALANCE

It seems that everyone is in a constant state of luxurious disrepair.
—*Six Degrees of Separation*

When John Paul Getty was asked, "How much is enough?" he replied, "Just a little bit more." Once you've achieved a certain degree of success, such questions do indeed arise. How far do you go? And according to what yardstick? The ability to answer these questions involves the cultivation of self-knowledge and a sense of balance. Not asking them at all can ultimately lead to extremism and even downfall.

Before we look at the potential negative tendencies and the tactics you can use to counteract them, let's consider how the current "work" culture is affecting individuals and organizations in North America and around the world.

According to the *Globe and Mail*, a 2001 National Work–Life Conflict Study found that "25 percent of Canadians worked at least 50 hours a week in 2001, which was up substantially from a decade earlier, when only 10 percent of workers reported such long hours." Similarly, a 1999 Conference Board of Canada report stated that "almost half of all Canadians are experiencing a moderate to high level of stress today as a result of trying to balance their work and home lives; ten years ago, only 27 percent felt this way." They also noted that "60 percent agreed with the statement that they don't have enough time for themselves."

This stress ultimately increases medical costs and decreases productivity for individuals and companies alike. In her 2002 book *The New Culture of Desire: Five Radical New Strategies That Will Change Your Business and Your Life,* Melinda Davis notes that the Centers for Disease Control and Prevention in the US "state unequivocally that 80 percent of our medical expenditures now are stress-related. . . . Seventy percent of Americans report high to moderate levels of stress at work, and one out of four . . . has felt 'stressed to the point of losing control by screaming and shouting' at work. Fully 98 percent of Americans believe that stress can make them sick. Stress, in fact, may cause their demise. 'Rage' is now the second leading cause of workplace mortality."

Workplace-induced stress and stress-related illness aren't limited to North America. An International Labour Organization report cites these figures:

- In Finland, more than 50 percent of the workforce experiences some kind of stress-related symptoms, such as anxiety, depressive feelings, physical pain, social exclusion, or sleep disorders.
- In Germany, the annual volume of production lost because of absenteeism related to mental health disorders was estimated at that time to be more than five billion deutsche marks annually.
- Public health statistics in Poland indicate that growing numbers of people—especially individuals suffering from

depressive disorders—are receiving mental health care, a trend that can be related to the country's socioeconomic transformation and resulting increases in unemployment, job insecurity, and declining living standards.

The costs incurred by what might be euphemistically referred to as "imbalance" are astronomical. In the US, clinical depression has become one of the most common illnesses; each year it affects one in ten working-age adults and results in a loss of approximately 200 million working days. And the International Labour Organization report estimates that in the European Union anywhere from 3 to 4 percent of gross national product (GNP) is spent on mental health problems. In many countries, early retirement due to mental health difficulties is increasing to the point where these difficulties are becoming the most common reason for allocating disability pensions.

> "The central motivating force of human behavior remains self-preservation, but it is now a sense of self-preservation that focuses on our inner and not our outer selves."

Given these grim statistics, it's not surprising that stress relief is by far the largest subcategory in the US$1 billion self-help book business, according to the research cited by Melinda Davis. "The central motivating force of human behavior remains self-preservation, but it is now a sense of self-preservation that focuses on our inner and not our outer selves . . . and 'a safe, happy home' and 'peace of mind' [are] at the top of aspirational lists once headed by house, cars, and the latest electronic equipment." Davis goes on to cite a study, conducted by the Next Group in the US, in which 76 percent of respondents said that mental illness or incapacity—their own or someone else's—was the greatest threat to their future, and 64 percent consider their "state of mind" to be a significant concern.

It's no wonder that I, like many of my peers and colleagues, spent the first twelve years of my career attempting to balance work and life. As a writer, speaker, and entrepreneur, I'm still struggling with balance issues, but I've since had the benefit of collecting a whole host of tactics and strategies from my clients and readers. In conducting the over thirty interviews for this book, I was happily surprised to find that many of the most insightful suggestions came from those who work in some of the most challenging industries, including journalism and the performing arts. I hope I can do justice to their words of wisdom.

DETERMINING HOW MUCH IS ENOUGH

I've read every one of Po Bronson's books, often nodding in agreement, having lived and breathed many of the moments he describes in such works as *Bombardiers*, *The First $20 Million Is Always the Hardest*, and *The Nudist on the Late Shift—And Other True Tales of Silicon Valley*. His latest bestseller, *What Should I Do with My Life?*, marks a distinct shift in his style and focus. Whereas his previous books looked at the powerful entrepreneurs in Silicon Valley, this one features interviews with hundreds of people from all walks of life about the inspiring journeys they've taken to find their calling. I began my interview with Po by asking him whether he thought there was such a thing as a balanced life. This was his response: "I came from the techie life—where the belief was that something worth doing must be worth doing all the time. . . . The notion was 'Go ahead and let your life become lopsided with passion.' This was really sort of an explicit end, and implicitly what people were looking for and hoping for in the high-tech world—business and intensity. But ultimately, it's naive to think that's sustainable. When things are going great, it works, but when things are really tough on the roller coaster of life, this is a very dangerous model."

I knew this firsthand. And it reminded me that if you want to proactively stave off imbalance, you need to acknowledge two realities: first, by signing up for ambition, any person's weakness is vulnerable to exploitation—people who have a tendency to drink or eat too much, for example, may or may not know when to stop; and second, ambitionists live and breathe along a whole spectrum of levels of passion and success. And at the extreme ends of the spectrum, of course, are the extreme pitfalls. The three tendencies that pose the greatest threat to balance are, in ascending order, addiction, alienation, and seclusion. Ironically, people are often most susceptible to these imbalances—you could think of them as "deaf spots"—when they're on the upswing, when their momentum is in full gear.

Here's a summary of the tactics you'll need to counteract each of these potential deaf spots:

Avoiding addiction For ambitionists, the greatest addictive threat is, of course, to ambition itself. Ironically, you can offset this by upping the ante on other aspects of life—family, volunteer work, other personal relationships—whose added responsibilities will oblige you to juggle the variables. The next step is to create a cross-over plan that anticipates life post-career and so will prevent you from becoming beholden to the success afforded by your current position. Finally, ambitionists constantly assess their decisions to make sure they're not falling prey to the inducements of short-term gain.

Avoiding alienation   When success becomes the most important element of our world, the tendency is to start believing in your own invincibility. As a result, you might let fall by the wayside those people who aren't immediately relevant or necessary to sustaining your success. Ambitionists fend off such potential alienation by allowing their experience to reshape their definition of success, by committing to the industry they belong to, by making a conscious effort to reach out to others, and by acknowledging that sacrifice is part of the balance equation.

Avoiding seclusion   The evolution from addiction to alienation, if unchecked, often leads to seclusion. This ineffective coping mechanism effectively shuts down outside distractions and influences, obliterating the perspective that's often needed most to get past a particularly difficult patch. Ambitionists find ways to compartmentalize their personal and vocational energy, widen their interests beyond their day-to-day challenges, and designate a person to whom they can turn when perspective begins to elude them.

On the face of it, these three deaf spots may seem far from your current world. But like all negative tendencies, they have a way of creeping up on you with unexpected speed. Only by recognizing their signs, and putting a few proactive measures into place, can you counteract their sometimes powerful impact.

Avoiding Addiction

Once you've built up career momentum, the success can be intoxicating—which explains why addiction to ambition is so prevalent today. What are the telltale signs? Whether you're a local business leader, a noted celebrity, or a rising careerist, the most obvious symptom is when you start believing your own press! Therapists, vocational counsellors, and personal coaches will tell you that people can see themselves as having a level of importance within their company or industry that's way beyond reality. Another common sign is what's referred to as "connection anxiety," whereby being away from a cellphone or BlackBerry produces enough anxiety to preclude getting anything else done. These people feel so instrumental to every play within a company or organization that they're unable to carve out time away from their work. It's an addictive lifestyle that's hard to break.

Ambition addiction occurs when people are so excited by their own success that they're unable to take a pause, reflect, and regain a larger perspective. Here's a case in point. In the 1950s a real estate company constructed a thousand buildings in a very short time. It became the first real estate company in Canada to get listed on the New York Stock Exchange. Everything was going well and its stock price was rising, but the company had some administrative issues that it hadn't looked after properly. In the end it suffered bad press and had to undergo SEC inquiries spurred on by competitors. I asked one of its founders why they didn't stop before it was too late. His response? "Because we were so damn exuberant and there was nothing like it."

> **Once you've built up career momentum, the success can be intoxicating—which explains why addiction to ambition is so prevalent today.**

Here are some of the ways to counteract addiction before it gets the better of you:

UP THE ANTE!

In the standard image of opera divas, "balance" isn't the first thing that comes to mind. But for Australian-born international opera star Cheryl Barker, balance is not only top of mind, it's a survival tactic. Cheryl has performed soprano roles in major opera houses all over the world, including the English National Opera, Scottish Opera, Vancouver Opera, De Vlaamse Opera, and Deutsche Opera Berlin. On one of my trips to London I was lucky enough to be able to chat with Cheryl just before she played the title role in Puccini's *Tosca* for the English National Opera. What I found was that despite her opera diva status, Cheryl is very focused and pragmatic about her work.

"My career has been a gradual buildup. This hasn't been an overnight career, so I've had time to watch and observe other people and how they handle their success. One of the biggest pitfalls I've found is that everything else seems to be ignored and sacrificed. One just has to look at someone like Maria Callas, who was tormented by a lack of balance. . . . In the opera world, one has a shelf life—and I think one must focus on the finish line and what you're going to do at the end of the career, when it gives *you* up! So many singers have sacrificed a family life to focus on their career, and then you see them lonely, sad figures at age fifty with no career or private life. It's a difficult decision, but I think it's so important to balance your career and private life, and to keep everything in perspective.

"I think having a baby has brought balance into my life because it demanded it. I have a three-year-old and I want to spend time with him, but at the same time I want him to be proud of me, and be a part of what I do. It's important that part of my identity is derived from my work. When I was younger, I spent a lot of time wondering and worrying about how my performances went. Now, I come home, put on my pajamas, eat toast, sip tea, play with my baby, and talk with my husband . . . that's equally important to me."

For many ambitionists in the early stages of their career, the thought of having to accommodate the responsibilities of family life seems counterproductive. But many people find that this added obligation fosters a balance that would otherwise escape them. Po Bronson's own experience bears this out. "I think I understood the issues a lot of these people I interviewed faced because I now have a young baby. In my early career I ruined a lot of the relationships in my life, because I sacrificed so much to become a writer and never took on the responsibility toward others that a child requires."

This is not to say that Cheryl and Po advocate having children as a guarantee for balance. But the responsibilities that come with being a parent are just one example of how adding a new element to life can become part of your purpose and your definition of ambition. Other ambitionists focus their attention on volunteer commitments that are deliberately unrelated to the work they do. I met one accountant who was taking her degree in law and had mapped out a pretty aggressive career plan for herself. In order to counteract her unwavering desire to achieve her career goals before she turned thirty-five, she signed up her dog for Therapy Dogs International and committed four hours a week to visiting hospitals, hospices, and children's care centers that benefited from regular visits from her dog. That was her version of creating balance.

Upping the ante on non-vocational responsibilities and priorities doesn't guarantee ego gratification—and that's just the point. When you succeed at work and are validated and applauded, you're motivated to return to the ring for more. Personal relationships and responsibilities, while rich and loving, don't always provide this immediate validation and will therefore furnish crucial perspective on whatever successes (and failures) occur in your working world.

CREATE RULES BEHIND THE SPONTANEITY

In the movie *Six Degrees of Separation* a teacher is asked, "How do you get grade twos to be such Picassos, such Miros?" "I don't have any secret," she replies. "I just know when to take their drawings away from them." This teacher could bring out the best in her students by setting some limits to their creativity. Likewise, the best way to determine what's enough and what's too much is to find the balance between structure and allow for a certain level of spontaneity—since, after all, spontaneity can open the door to serendipity, timing, and luck.

As a top financial consultant puts it, "You have to be actionable to your values at all times. Sure, you can have short-term, extreme pressures that you have to get through, but it's easier to know that you'll always have touchstones that bring you back to reality—like staying in touch with your loved ones once a day, building fitness into your schedule even when you're on the road, and remembering to contribute to charitable organizations no matter how busy or how important you think you are. Just as you choose to give in to anger, I believe that you can also choose to give in to imbalance."

Another important way to establish a structure for yourself is to take the long view and build in a cross-over plan for way down the road. I turn to the world of ballet by way of example.

Chan Hon Goh has been a principal dancer for the National Ballet of Canada since 1994. I was able to steal forty-five minutes from her between rehearsals at Toronto's National Ballet studio. During this brief interview—as she ate her lunch, kept her legs and toes wrapped for warmth, and answered my questions—I came to understand how this lovely, articulate prima ballerina has proven herself not only as a dancer, but also as an entrepreneur and role model for young dancers worldwide.

As the first Asian principal dancer to be hired by the National Ballet, Chan has worked very hard to achieve balance in an industry and art form that demands excess—in ability, commitment, and sheer stamina. Born in China, the only child of two professional ballet dancers, she grew up surrounded by discipline, hard work, and artistic endeavor. Her parents thought she had good potential as a concert pianist, so she spent her early years seated at the piano. When her parents moved to Canada and started a dance school in Vancouver, Chan began taking classes at the age of nine, mostly as a function of hanging around their studio. But once she started, there was no looking back: "I loved the dancing. I loved the integration between the music and the movement, and I loved being able to come outside myself, to explore, to be the temperament of the music or the movement, whether adagio or legato—to be able to interpret that. It almost allowed me to be another being."

With that kind of passion tucked into her tutu, Chan convinced her parents that she needed to work at dance seriously. At sixteen she won a full scholarship at the Prix de Lausanne in Switzerland, and two years later, in 1994, she was asked to join the National Ballet of Canada. She's been a principal dancer ever since.

Over the years and with the guidance of her parents, Chan has learned the value of balance in a world that forces its participants to focus entirely on themselves. "It's so easy to believe that nothing outside of your dancing matters, but if you don't ensure that you have a life outside the studio, you'll be unable to function in the real world."

How does that translate for Chan? A realistic acceptance that she can't be a prima ballerina her whole life. Like Cheryl Barker, she too will grow out of her spotlight—and she chooses to talk about it "out loud" as a means of accepting the inevitable. Chan has already put a cross-over plan into action, and is building the necessary stepping stones to segue into another, complementary career when her role as a principal dancer inevitably ends. Six years ago she and her husband launched Principal Dance Supplies, a company that manufactures shoes and other accessories for professional dancers and dance students. With Chan's firsthand experience and direct input from other dancers, combined with her husband's creative and business abilities, they've developed their company into a full-fledged business. As well, she recently released her autobiography and is working on opportunities that may be derived from that publishing venture. Her timing is canny: "I wanted to write a book that would speak to young girls when I was at the height of my career so that they could see me as a dancer on stage, relate it to the person writing the book, and be inspired by it." Chan's cross-over planning at the height of her success reflects the wisdom behind momentum building that I talked about in Rule 4: building your portfolio when you're at your busiest, and with the benefit of all that power and motivation backing you up.

GET PAST THE ECSTASY

At one point or another in our lives, many of us realize that we're making decisions based solely on satisfying such immediate desires as money, power, and recognition. When that happens, the ambitionists among us take the time to sit down and ask the following three questions: What am I most afraid of losing? What am I most addicted to? What am I least good at? *Honestly* answering these questions means facing your own limitations—and recognizing the importance of creating a realistic decision-making process. Hilary Brown, top foreign correspondent at ABC television, believes wholeheartedly in this philosophy. She learned the importance of what she calls "building upon the reality factor" the hard way.

Hilary started out doing freelance radio reports for CBC Radio in Paris; within a year she had joined its Paris bureau. Her first job in television came two years after that, at CBC Montreal. She had always wanted to be a broadcaster, and was particularly drawn to the role of foreign correspondent. "I think my voice and compassion for the victims of injustice are probably my best qualities," she notes. "I can also write a grammatical sentence."

Hilary's hard-knocks lesson in maintaining balance came a few years later. "My worst setback was accepting an assignment for which I was completely unqualified—that of Pentagon correspondent for NBC News. But because I was ambitious, I thought I could do it—so that wasn't really ambition so much as hubris. They thought I'd be gangbusters at the Pentagon because I was quite a good foreign correspondent, and I proved them wrong, an unforgivable sin. I went from being

> **"Dreams are like children, and it's wrong to burden them with too high expectations, too early, too young. Rather, tend to them and nurture them—your dreams, that is—which is a longer, sustainable approach to success."**

one of their best correspondents to a 'un-person' in the space of about four months. I got back on my horse by leaving the network and returning to my old network [ABC], which was where I belonged anyway."

There is no question that addiction—whether physical, emotional, or intellectual—is not an easy imbalance factor to contend with. Again, perspective is key to battling this lifelong temptation. If you look at your dreams with a certain level of distance, then you can learn to incorporate your passion ahead of time and plan accordingly. Po Bronson sums up the message succinctly: "Dreams are like children, and it's wrong to burden them with too high expectations, too early, too young. Rather, tend to them and nurture them—your dreams, that is—which is a longer, sustainable approach to success." It's also what allows ambitionists to get past the ecstasy.

Avoiding Alienation

Alienation has long been cited as the epitome of loneliness in twenty-first-century North American society. The word may evoke images of lone men and women sitting at their computers at night, trying to connect to some stranger digitally, or elderly people at their kitchen table, eating dinner alone. But, ironically, alienation is also a by-product of success and can affect those who are constantly surrounded by others. In fact, the more you succeed, the more susceptible you are to its shadow.

Alienation is usually associated with those in a leadership role who begin to believe that they're more capable than they really are and, based on their own self-aggrandizement, allow this belief to create a division between themselves and their employees and teammates. With this kind of self-imposed separation, when they go back to the drawing board looking for someone to discuss their ideas with, there's no one there. Similar to the addict's connection anxiety discussed above, the alienated person is the one who's likely to arrive at a family function and spend the entire time on her cellphone or waiting for an important email message. Or it may be the executive who shows up at a company retreat with his laptop and answers his emails in the midst of a group brainstorming session.

You can see how quickly addiction ("I can't stop working") can lead to alienation ("even when I'm interacting with people, I'm working at something else"). But the ambitionist relies on several ways to counteract this tendency:

REDEFINE YOUR WORK BASED ON WHO YOU'VE BECOME

One of the best ways to counteract potential alienation is to incorporate your unique perspective into the task at hand. Chan puts it eloquently: "This art form [dance] can be so deep—it's endless and limitless and only a function of how much you're willing to put into it. Each time I come back to a role, I always add my current life experiences into my interpretation of the character and the steps. I allow the music to speak differently to me, and depending on where I am in my life, I'm able to see where the correspondence between me and that certain character lies."

This same philosophical approach is reflected in Po Bronson's research. "Often people learn from their experiences, but their behavior patterns lag behind. The conventional thought process is that you just have to make it through the hard times, to cope and to get things back to where they were . . . but if instead you could learn from your setbacks and embrace the sadness or grief, etc., and incorporate it into your current work, then you're constantly ensuring that you're in touch with the real world, not working on a figment of your own desires."

By allowing the time for self-reflection, even while riding high on a wave of success, ambitionists challenge themselves to assess what and who is contributing to their success at any given point. And this constant redefinition of their efforts in the context of who they are can offset the grandiose inclinations that are so symptomatic of alienation.

COMMIT TO FULL PARTICIPATION

Being connected—to your community as well as to your field of work—is simply a realistic approach to building ambition. Elitism and exclusivity, after all, are really means of protecting those who aren't willing to be jostled by the rough and tumble of the world outside their microcosm. Any industry demands our full participation, and the ambitionists among us step up to the plate without reservation.

Part of accepting this responsibility is acknowledging the rules of engagement. Here are a few recommendations:

Good manners Hilary Brown believes that one of the most important elements for long-term success is good manners. From the way you answer your telephone or sever an important supplier relationship to the way you acknowledge others' contribution, etiquette is essential. Simple, but easy to forget when your success precedes you.

Genuine listening In any organization where individuals' talents and contributions are scrutinized daily and the pressure is intense, the ability to listen can make the difference between group success and ineffectiveness. Giving people's actions the benefit of the doubt, learning to cultivate real friendships, and genuinely listening to the input of others are all key to ongoing group harmony.

Fighting in good temper People like to challenge success; it's a natural human instinct. Ambitionists learn early on that it's not only how you win, but how you lose that people remember. You can have a disagreement at the boardroom table and shake hands at an evening function later the same day; you can have artistic differences in the studio but dance magnificently as a team for your audience. Alienating those you beat does not bode well, but even more important, alienating those you lose to leaves you open to unnecessary seclusion.

One of the patterns that emerged from the interviews I conducted for this book was that commitment to one's métier and industry is essential. By embracing the responsibilities of belonging and participating within an industry, a community, or a company, each of these ambitionists learned to build bridges to others. This is a core value that becomes even more important the more successful you become.

KNOW WHAT TO SACRIFICE

Ambitionists are pragmatists with vision, so it's not surprising that they can discern the potential for alienation, try to keep it at bay, and focus on *choice* as the operative word when maintaining the precarious balance that their personal and work lives demand. And sometimes it's only when you lose that balance that the power of sacrifice hits home.

> **Ambitionists are pragmatists with vision, so it's not surprising that they can discern the potential for alienation, try to keep it at bay, and focus on *choice* as the operative word.**

"You could argue that if you're too balanced, and

too happy, you aren't actually achieving as much," muses Hilary Brown. "I would guess that most very successful people don't have a balanced life because they simply don't have the time, or because they're driven. A demanding career is just that: demanding. If you're very ambitious you'll sacrifice a personal life—having children, for example—because you might not succeed in your career if you don't.

"But if you want to achieve balance, you may find yourself passing up the big assignments, for instance, so that you can be home for this birthday or that family holiday. I once gave up Christmas with my husband and small son for an overseas assignment—because of my ambition—but I felt miserable. I carried out the assignment and actually built up quite a head of steam—what you'd call 'momentum'—and produced some pretty good reports. But ultimately, when I look back on it now, what did it give me in the end, what did it prove?"

Hilary weighed the sacrifice she'd have to make and still chose to take the overseas assignment, knowing that in order to succeed she'd have to live with that sacrifice. Conversely, at other times in her career she might have weighed the sacrifices associated with turning down professional opportunities, and opted for more life balance.

Sacrifice, whether it's on the personal or the work side of the equation, is an inevitable corollary of ambition. Ambitionists allow themselves to try out their comfort level with various kinds of sacrifice, knowing they have a choice every step of the way. And when they make major decisions, they always try to minimize who they alienate by including them in their ongoing efforts to maintain balance. Ultimately, it's the difference between admiring ambition for what it provides us and idolizing it by allowing it to take over.

Avoiding Seclusion

The chronological buildup from addiction to alienation, if unchecked, often leads to seclusion, the third deaf spot. Successful—often highly successful—people who are addicted to ambition may start to limit their activities to those within the work realm, distancing themselves from those whom they might think of as peripheral associations. If this continues for long enough, self-aggrandizement takes over and a self-imposed process of seclusion sets in. The process may begin by secluding oneself from certain people, but it often extends to seclusion from situations, important decisions, and physical settings—and ultimately from their lifework itself.

Seclusion often follows the alienation stage after either a long run of too much success at one time or an unexpected setback. In the latter case, instead of sitting back and re-evaluating their goals or seeking helpful guidance from team members and champions, people simply give in to fear and disappear from the scene.

DESIGN YOUR TIME

In the attempt to pre-empt any potential seclusionary tendencies, the element of time—how you spend, value, categorize, and rationalize it—must inevitably come into play. Wayne Scott, executive coach at Toronto's Action Strategies Inc., is often called upon to help his clients effectively manage their time. "Time management is such an overused term. But in the context of alienation or seclusion, it's essential to move toward something rather than carving out escape routes from the very work that's challenging you. Defining how you divide your time is really a way of designing your time rather than finding ways to move away from your day-to-day responsibilities. It's a subtle distinction, but it can make all the difference."

Here's a simple exercise that Wayne uses to help his clients prioritize and redesign their time. Choose three or four major categories in your life (work, family, personal time, and community). For at least one week (preferably a month), determine how you're spending your days and assign them to each of these categories. As you review your week, it will become quite evident where the imbalance lies, and this will help you to decide how to reassign your energy and time accordingly. For example, if it turns out that what you're calling family time is actually spent picking up the dry cleaning and buying groceries, perhaps it would be better to, say, use an online grocery service and spend that time with your family members instead.

Here are other tactics that ambitionists rely on:

SIDE TIME In *The New Culture of Desire,* Melinda Davis cites the tendency to "rush to personal betterment" through seminars, self-help books, and even a hot new trend in travel called "Skill Collectors," whereby "you don't just come home with a tan, you come back with a performance skill from speed reading to self-hypnosis." Though this might appeal to the ambitionist's overachieving predisposition, it doesn't provide the kind of relief from performance, goal setting, and focused activities that's so integral to those with a hectic schedule.

One way to engage the pause button is to integrate your desire to spend time with family and friends by setting a simple yet doable goal. For example, one executive and mother of a five-year-old complained that although she saw her son at the end of her long workday, she missed actually doing an activity with him—an important value she wanted to pass on. Rather than setting an unrealistic goal such as taking him to soccer practice twice a week, she decided to get a tandem bike that she and her son could ride together—a favorite sport of his. It soon became part of her routine for the two to ride it to the subway a few times a week. While it meant having her husband change his morning routine slightly, this executive found that the time she valued with her son was integrated into her workday. The simplicity of the goal and the integration of the activity were key to giving this executive meaningful side time.

DIVERSIFICATION We've often heard that it's not how much you make but how you spend it that matters. The same is true with ambition and success. If you're successful only in your particular area and haven't taken any time to incorporate other ideas, culture, arts, books, sports, or charity work into your world, the quality of your success is ultimately diminished. Many of the people I've interviewed over the years spoke of their dedication to being a true Renaissance person whose interests are many and varied. By relinquishing some of the control and single-minded dedication to your work, you not only offset potential seclusion but also move toward a more all-encompassing definition of success. And that may offer new frontiers for harnessing your ambition in later years. In fact, many successful ambitionists go on to dedicate themselves to altruistic endeavors later in life, a happy development that we'll talk about in Rule 7.

> **If you're successful only in your particular area and haven't taken any time to incorporate other ideas, culture, arts, books, sports, or charity work into your world, the quality of your success is ultimately diminished.**

The reality is that there are certain times—at the outset of your career, or at a particularly crucial turning point—when you have to pay your dues and when branching out isn't an option. You work the extra time, you put in the extra effort, and you gain the advantage you think you need to succeed according to your own meter. But at some point ambitionists find a way to move on from this lopsided model and incorporate a wider range of experiences, ideas, and pursuits—and a means of truly designing their ambition.

SAVIORS AND CONFESSORS One of the best ways to ensure that you avoid seclusion is to choose a designated savior or confessor. In the belonging stage you created a team of champions, momentum builders, and leveragers, and designating a savior or confessor is simply an extension of this process. A savior needs to be someone you trust and respect, usually someone who's had more success, failures, and all-around experience than you. This is the person you can send a quick question to by email, meet for lunch, or ask to be present at an important business meeting so that he or she can give you a trusted opinion. If it's a confessor you're looking for, then you simply need an exceptional listener. Either way, by setting up a mentoring relationship with this person in advance, you'll know you can rely on him or her when the chips are down.

Conversely, it's also important to relinquish those relationships that might be toxic for you—those individuals, for example, who promote extremism and ignore the downside of long-term imbalance. Misery loves company, so those who have slipped into addictive, alienating, or reclusive tendencies may even advocate this state to you. Chan Hon Goh talks about this in the context of her world: "Generally, I've been able to block the bad people out of my life, and this has made me able to keep my faith in human nature. I've found that I surround myself not only with those people who love and care for me, but also older and wiser people who provide guidance and influence—by example. In the world of dance, which can be so single-minded, this has been key for creating a life outside the studio and a bridge to creating a cross-over to life after dance."

Setting up a personal board of directors is one tactic that many ambitionists use to create the mentoring relationships they require. Many such programs are aimed at guiding entrepreneurs, but the concept can be extended to accommodate a number of vocational scenarios. For a fee, there are consultants who specialize in matching people up with business experts, personal advisers, spiritual mentors, and those who are well connected in particular fields. These consultants meet with their clients regularly to help them create a life plan. Regardless of your business or career, working with a single individual or a personal board is an excellent way to build in a support mechanism. Not only will it help you avoid any seclusionary tendencies, but along the way your career will undoubtedly benefit from the added experience and expertise.

A FINAL WORD

When you come down to it, one of the primary reasons people long for a certain level of success is the freedom it affords them. That's why some choose time off over money, or a flexible schedule over status. The important point here is that you have to constantly step back and redefine what freedom means for you. To stay in balance you need to stay current with who you really are and what you really want. Otherwise, you may find yourself replaying an outdated tape. You may be making piles of money, for example, but you no longer feel like getting out of bed in the morning because you're working more than you really want to. By constantly taking a realistic, unemotional inventory of what you value, and by measuring your own definition of ambition on a regular basis, you'll minimize the tendency to fall prey to addiction, alienation, or seclusion.

"How to Lead a Rich Life," the same *Fast Company* article that I quoted from in Rule 4, has this to say about what constitutes true wealth: "The two things that wealthy people devote more time and energy to than financial planning are spending time with their children or grandchildren and entertaining close friends. They spend significantly more time on a rich mix of people-centric leisure activities each month than on big-ticket items. . . . Every time I talk to these people, it's the same thing: 'I love my life. I love my wife. I can't wait to get to work in the morning.' And that, folks, is as rich as the rich life gets." The same equation applies to the ambitionist: from the discipline of creating a balance between work and life comes the freedom to love both.

> **To stay in balance you need to stay current with who you really are and what you really want. Otherwise, you may find yourself replaying an outdated tape.**

In my attempt to define balance, I asked all those I interviewed whether they thought the ambitionist was one who "had it all" or one who was able to "juggle it all." One interviewee said it best: "Ambition isn't really about having it all *or* juggling it all, but truly about *wanting* it all." If that's true, then balance comes from minimizing the shadow side of the "wanting" part while attempting to get closer to the "all."

Of all my interviews on the subject of balance, one in particular stays with me. Perhaps it's my own love of wine and wine collecting, and perhaps it's the romantic life of an Italian vintner, but Silvia Imparato's story continues to resonate.

Silvia was a portrait photographer in Rome. She loved photography, she loved wine, and her grandparents owned twenty-seven hectares of land close to Salerno in southern Italy where they grew fruits and nuts. But somehow, she never put all these things together.

One day in 1985 she was doing a portrait of an American who happened to be a wine connoisseur. He invited Silvia to a wine club meeting that evening at a local Enoteca in Rome, where she met a number of wine lovers and wine specialists. Among them was someone who had worked with the famous wine producer Piero Antinori, and this man encouraged her to think about producing wine on her family property. By the end of that year, to everyone's surprise, this risk-taking photographer had partnered with two industry experts and begun planting grapes for Montevetrano Wines.

Unfortunately, Silvia's partnership didn't last past the six-month mark, and she suddenly found herself running a small winery with no knowledge and no support. But what she lacked in experience she made up for in desire, passion, and a love of wine. While continuing to support herself with portrait photography and using the labor of local townspeople, she worked with a small team and planted, stored, corked, distributed, and marketed a very small production through sheer love of the wine, love of the land, and a strong, ambitious nature. By 1993 they had produced three thousand bottles and were getting a great response.

As with most ambitionists, after a few years Silvia wanted to move her business to the next level. So she took a chance and sent a few bottles to the world-renowned wine taster and critic Robert

Parker. "I was still doing photos in my studio in Rome at the time. One afternoon between photo sessions I see this fax coming through—hand-written and signed by Robert Parker. It said something like, 'Your wine is fantastic and I want to tell you that I've chosen to write an article about it in my next issue.' I thought it was a prank from one of my friends. But it wasn't! Parker gave my wine a tremendous rating, and within a month I could barely keep up with the demand. Buyers thought I was playing hard to get, when really I was simply unable to keep up with customer requests. The result was that the price of my wine kept going higher and higher, and today I produce twenty-five thousand bottles per year and compete on an international level."

Yes, this is a romantic story—an ambitionist's fairy tale, if you will. But in the context of balance, it's a fable. Another twenty minutes into our interview and Silvia is talking about the strain the business puts on her life: the time she has to spend, the learning she has to do, the day-to-day issues she has to tackle on her own. But in the same breath, she marvels at her achievements within a competitive, labor-intensive, male-dominated field.

"What is my ambition? To make the best wine possible. What is my life about? It's about finding the balance between the earthly delights of being outdoors, working with the earth, the sun, and the rain, hiring local townspeople and training them in ways they never thought possible. But ultimately, I find balance when I sit under an olive tree at the end of a long day and taste the wine I've created with my daughter."

Ambitious? Yes. But one that defines a happy balance simply by wanting it all.

RULE 6
MATURITY

Only those who dare to fail greatly can ever achieve greatly.
—*Robert F. Kennedy*

Failure for the ambitionist is like death and taxes: it's inevitable and no one gets away from it. Rule 6 is relatively straightforward. It's about failure. Or rather, it's about how the ambitionist views failure, deals with setbacks and, most important, recognizes that it's the ability to bounce back time and again that's the mark of maturity.

Over the years, whenever I've had the opportunity to interview or chat with those who have gained enormous success in their lives, I'm always happily surprised to hear them recount their failures as being a major contribution to their ultimate achievements. More than that, these failed endeavors are worn as a badge of honor. In the words of Havelock Ellis, "It is on our failures that we base a new and different and better success."

Maturity is a place you choose to get to. It's based on an ability to manage your reactions to situations, and it comes as a result of experiences that are often out of your control. And it begins with the recognition that by embracing failure and focusing on bounce-back, you'll go on to further and often greater success. The story that Michael Birch told me makes a good starting point for any ambitionist ready to embrace Rule 6.

> **Maturity is a place you choose to get to. It's based on an ability to manage your reactions to situations, and it comes as a result of experiences that are often out of your control.**

Imagine growing up on a remote island six hundred miles northeast of Winnipeg, across the water from a reserve with a population of fifteen hundred people. You spend your winters almost entirely in seclusion, staying in a log cabin with just your brother for company, unable to congregate or even communicate with friends on the other side of the water. What would you do? If you were Michael Birch, you'd dream and wonder how you were going to be sure that you'd find a way to surround yourself with people—always.

The influence of a British father and a First Nations mother taught Michael two things: from his father, a pilot, he learned that he should never work for someone else but try to live his dream and do it on his own. From his mother, he got a sense of commitment, determination, and willpower.

Michael quit school after grade ten, intent on becoming a successful entrepreneur. He decided to run a convenience store and built up a fairly successful business. But it wasn't successful enough for him. He looked around and, despite his lack of education, had the wherewithal to recognize a major gap in the market: First Nations people drank cola. In fact, they drank more cola than most Canadians—at a rate of 4 to 1 they were the fastest-growing sector of consumers around. There were 620 reserves in Canada with limited access and a welcome audience. Why not create a cola just for them? And so, Michael created First Nations Cola. He got Cott Beverages to do the bottling, had a line on distribution, and was hauling cases of his new beverage to the reserves as fast as he could.

And with it he enjoyed more attention from media and his community than he'd ever dreamed of. Michael was riding high—at least for a few years—until the competitive nature of the business caught up with him. The major players in the cola market had volume and clout, making it very difficult for Michael to get proper shelf space for his product. The immense production of the larger companies allowed them to make a higher profit margin per case than Michael could ever hope to squeeze out of his small output. And, to his dismay, although First Nations people drank a lot of pop, they're also more brand loyal than most and weren't going to easily switch their drink of preference.

At twenty-seven, despite numerous attempts to find a way to stay afloat, Michael had to close shop. He's quick to say that he never went belly up but negotiated with his creditors to pay them over a period of time. All in all, though, he lost the business as well as $1 million in cash. He had hit bottom. He was cash poor, sixty-five pounds overweight, and had turned to alcohol. In short, he'd lost his sense of purpose and was on a slippery slope downward. "I felt sorry for myself. I couldn't figure out why I failed. Was it because I had no education? Was it because I didn't have a knack for business? Or was it bad luck?" And he kept cycling through the refrain.

One day his assistant turned to him and said, "Michael. That's enough. What kind of legacy are you going to leave your kids? Are they going to remember you as the guy who gave up after one failed attempt? If so, then they'll only remember you as a quitter." It was his wakeup call. In Michael's words, "That was enough to get me up off my ass and start again." A quick trip to the mall, a haircut later, a new pair of jeans and a new attitude, and he was ready to start again.

After much thought, he realized that his original instinct for combining the buying power of a group as big as the First Nations was dead on, though maybe his product focus was not. If he could apply what he learned from the failure of his first venture, there was no reason why he couldn't use his model more strategically. This time it was an offering rather than a product, together with a plan for what is now known as the First Nations Buying Group. By combining the buying power of the First Nations reserves, Michael was able to attract large corporations that wanted to sell their products and services at a competitive rate to First Nations people. They offered lower prices for everything from toys to telephone bills to computer equipment, and in turn they received exclusivity for their product category.

Michael began his new venture in Manitoba. By cutting a collective deal with Manitoba Telecom Services to reduce the average cost of long-distance calls from 18 to 7.5 cents a minute, he started the ball rolling. Today, about half of the reserves in Manitoba, the Maritimes, and Ontario are on board, and he won't stop until he has them all. What's more, Michael's product lineup now includes Toys R Us, Grand & Toy, Xerox, Bell Ontario, and an insurance company, all under one pricing banner.

I have no doubt that Michael will go on to succeed in whatever endeavors he chooses. Yes, he may fail again, as we all do—but he now has the experience and maturity to pick himself back up.

BOUNCING BACK FROM FAILURE

Maturity is gained by the ability to identify and accept failure for what it is and no more. The internal dialogue is not "I'm a failure. I'm not ambitious. I can't succeed" but rather "In my ambitious journey, I've had a failure. Out of this failure I'm going to learn what I'm good at and how I'm going to move forward."

Thomas A. Edison said, "I have not failed. I've just found ten thousand ways that won't work." Here's an overview of the five key strategies that help to foster a mature attitude and allow ambitionists to use failure as a catalyst for future success:

Embracing rejection A necessary part of the road to success—and one of the cornerstones of the ambitionist's portfolio—is rejection. Rather than allowing it to deflate you, embrace it as a means for propelling yourself forward with more resolve.

Taking a realistic inventory Now that you've dealt with the ebbs and flows that come with momentum and struggled with the potential threats to a balanced life, you're ready to realistically reassess your skills in relation to the market conditions that most affect your lifework. Accepting your strengths and weaknesses will help you bounce back from setbacks with greater speed and accuracy.

Fostering your curiosity People often allow the pressures of family, peers, and society to influence their decisions about their lifework. If a specific vocational choice isn't applauded by those they care about, they're often tempted to divert their efforts. But choosing respectability, power, or status, for example, over the calling of true ambition will rarely sustain the ambitionist's interest.

Focusing on serial bounce-back It's not how high you jump but rather how quickly you rebound when you hit bottom. Mature ambitionists focus their energy on what I call "serial bounce-back"—the ability to recover from setbacks many times.

Building character By embracing rejection and committing to bounce back on a regular basis, ambitionists are really building strength of character. Understanding how fear, choice, responsibility, power, and performance all play a role helps create a mature approach to both success and failure.

In the ambitious journey, some of the seven rules require a more tactical approach than others. Maturity, however, is more a function of reflection and perspective. As such, it begins with the right mindset and then moves on from there.

Embracing Rejection

Walt Disney said, "You may not realize it when it happens, but a kick in the teeth may be the best thing in the world for you." Michael Birch would likely agree. **If you look around you, the people who are most ambitious and most successful are often the first ones to admit to the many failures they've experienced along the way.** Take Steve Fossett, for example, a balloonist featured in *Vanity Fair*. This fifty-eight-year-old options trader failed five times in his attempt to achieve the first solo round-the-world balloon flight. His failures (which included plummeting 29,000 feet into the Coral Sea) only fired up his sole goal: "personal achievement based on skill and effort." By defining success on these terms, Fossett embraces Henry Ford's notion that "failure is only the opportunity to begin again more intelligently."

I've received many emails from readers across the board who have related stories about how they persevered in the face of rejection. One woman told me that she decided she wanted to get her PhD at a later stage in life. Despite excellent marks, references, and work-related experience, she had to apply to the university of her preference six times before they finally accepted her. Each time she was rejected, however, she told me that she chose to focus on how much she'd learn about herself if she overcame it. At the same time, she knew that she was building up the necessary calluses to deal with any bigger failures that might come her way.

To build anything worthwhile takes time. To establish a business, for example, most experienced business operators will tell you that it takes a minimum of ten years to truly succeed, and that rejection is an inevitable part of the journey. For writers, rejection is a veritable cornerstone. One tactic that helps many writers is to immediately dive into a new project as soon as they send off their current material for consideration. Not only does this reconfirm their ambition in the process; it also lessens the blow should their material be turned down.

Taking a Realistic Inventory

In the momentum stage I talked about the importance of keeping just enough distance between you and the decisions you make as a means of pacing yourself. And now, when you turn to the pragmatic exercise of realistically assessing your strengths, that crucial sense of perspective comes into play again. This will enable you to move on from any given setback, since rather than simply compensating for your weaknesses you'll be truly using your strengths. The ideas of Robert Fritz provide an interesting perspective on success and failure.

Fritz is a pioneer of human development and author of *The Path of Least Resistance,* in which he takes his experience as a musician and applies it to the creative and working process in general. In my conversations with consultants and vocational coaches, Fritz's approach to understanding failure and rejection has come up time and again. Executive coach Wayne Scott has often found Fritz's thinking helpful in understanding and moving beyond failure. "From my experience, lots of people avoid rejection as much as possible. It's really a human tendency. But rather than simply build up a system to avoid rejection, which is inevitable, I turn to Robert Fritz's approach, which is based on taking a realistic inventory before you approach rejection and failure. Let's take a salesperson, for example, which is someone who needs to deal with rejection on a regular basis. According to Fritz, you need to ask yourself two important questions. The first question is Why would I make a sales call at the risk of being rejected? In order to answer this question, you have to acknowledge that you may never learn to like a certain aspect of your work or even be very good at it, but you can learn to cope with this part of your job because you're doing it in order to achieve a larger goal—in this case, to sell successfully. So, if your fear of rejection is more important

Although inspiration is a starting point, in most endeavors it's the discipline and maturity that enable us to make it to the finish line.

than the idea of succeeding as a salesperson, you may want to reconsider being a salesperson. Hence, you're realistically assessing your skills.

"If, on the other hand, you don't have this fear, then merely acknowledge that you don't like rejection and give yourself permission *not* to have to spend more energy than necessary convincing yourself that you enjoy that part of your job—just do it. By realistically identifying where you sit in relation to the element of rejection that's part of your job description, you emotionally detach yourself from something that's counterintuitive and you reduce the added pressure of potentially failing at it."

What I like best about this kind of pragmatic thinking is that you avoid getting caught in unrealistic—and emotionally charged—expectations of success and failure. Fritz's approach reminds us that although inspiration is a starting point, in most endeavors it's the discipline and maturity that enable us to make it to the finish line. In the vast majority of things in life, there will be some parts that you don't enjoy but that come with the territory. It's the passion that generates the vision—and so, while you have to be passionate about what it is that you want to create, you don't need that same level of intensity about all the steps involved to get there.

Bob Faulkner—one of the oldest and best adventure racers around—has made his mark using this approach to realistic inventory taking. When he was in his mid-forties, with a growing printing business as well as real estate and other ongoing ventures, he had little time for athletics of any kind. Nonetheless, a friend approached him to be his support team for the Iron Man contest in Penticton, BC. "I was smoking two packs a day, sixty pounds overweight, and a social drinker. Basically, I was a forty-six-year-old going to hell." But the Iron Man race transformed him. He saw people who had applied incredible discipline to enter the race and thought that if he put his mind to it, he could be one of them. "Today," Bob says, "I compete around the world in adventure racing and I pull my weight with the best of them. By honestly looking at my strengths—determination, drive, maturity—and weaknesses—not a great athlete, older, and not as strong as others—I'm able to succeed." Today, Bob is fifty-six years old and competes with athletes around the world who are half his age and have double his ability.

Taking a realistic inventory works for companies and organizations too, of course. Say a group of executives get together to set goals based on their individual MBOs (management by objectives) or other prescribed targets. Once the goals are established these executives will generally swing right into action. Yet these aims are often based on the mistaken assumption that everyone at the table has the same perspective on where the company is at, its strengths and weaknesses. And so, while the resulting action plan might be very precise, it won't accommodate the varied views of the decision makers at the table. If a company is planning to expand into a new market, for example, and the engineering department feels that the weak link is in distribution and the salespeople feel the weak link is in the new product specs and the operations executives are solely focused on the lack of reporting structure within the company, then the inventory of strengths and weaknesses is so diverse that no action plan will be able to address all perspectives. If, instead, the group hears out each person and comes to a consensus on the company's assets, strengths, and market conditions *prior* to developing an action plan, their potential for success is all the greater.

Fostering Your Curiosity

While the first two strategies rely on pragmatism, the third strategy asks ambitionists to refocus on what gets them going, what excites them most, what arouses their curiosity. When I set out to research the importance of maturity in the context of ambition, curiosity wasn't the first theme that came to mind. But after I'd interviewed a number of people, it became apparent that curiosity is, after all, really a reflection of your interests and your passions. Nurturing it, then, will make failure that much easier to get over.

> **People who stay open to their own curiosity are often able to tap into what they truly care about. Though it may take time to find the right vocational fit, when they do they can take in stride the successes and failures along the way.**

Many people deny their curiosity and desires, and look to respectability as a surrogate for self-fulfillment. Whether they come to this decision based on outside influences or from a need to gain external validation, these people tend to be highly competitive. They measure themselves against others rather than finding their own definition of worthwhile ambition and self-fulfillment, and hence they're rarely satisfied for long. People who stay open to their own curiosity, however, are often able to tap into what they truly care about. Though it may take time to find the right vocational fit, when they do they can take in stride the successes and failures along the way.

To quote Samuel Johnson, "Curiosity is, in great and generous minds, the first passion and the last." And so it is that Dr. Susan S. Lieberman, director of the Species Programme at the World Wildlife Fund International, has never strayed from her own curiosity. Between a field trip to Nepal, where she was involved in a major rhino translocation, and a research excursion to Africa, I was able to grab a half hour with Dr. Lieberman on the phone. Here is her story:

As a kid, Susan was always interested in animals and wildlife. In her family, if you were good at science you went into medicine, but she somehow convinced her parents that biology would be a better degree for her. After receiving her PhD, a fellowship that took her to the coast of Costa Rica provided a pivotal moment: "There I sat for two hours alone in a rainforest and I was overwhelmed by the place. To me, the diversity was grand and I knew that I had to do work on biodiversity—something to do with conservation. My curiosity was ignited and I couldn't ignore my interest in this kind of work—right from the get-go.

"But in keeping with the academia model that was drilled into me, I went about looking for academic jobs, thinking that I'd have to somehow swallow my curiosity for the broader issues in order to pursue a subject that I loved. After much reflection, I allowed myself to move away from what was expected of me and responded to a job to do policy work for the Humane Society. And it was like a dream come true. I loved negotiation, loved policy, and found a meaningful niche for myself in Washington."

Eventually Susan got a job with the US government working on CITES (Convention on International Trade in Endangered Species) policy. She was instrumental in implementing the ivory trade ban, lobbied against whaling, and worked on a 1992 law to ban the wild bird trade in the US. When she decided to live in Europe, it was a natural evolution for her to move from government work to an organization like WWF. Today, on behalf of the WWF, Susan coordinates all the global policy work on CITES and endangered species. These include elephants, pandas, tigers, and gorillas—what are referred to as the flagship species whose conservation is essential to and indicative of healthy ecosystems.

Susan's seasoned ability to negotiate, communicate with the media, and help set policy was all made possible by that decision she made years ago in the Costa Rica rainforest. By fostering her curiosity and not giving in to someone else's version of a respectable job, she's been able to deal with the setbacks and successes as part of the ambitious journey she has chosen. "When I was quoted in *Time* magazine," she said, laughing, "my mother finally forgave me for not becoming a doctor!" In the end, the respect and approval that come from others (and to which we're all susceptible) take a backseat to her own sense of accomplishment.

Focusing on Serial Bounce-Back

Like many people, I've always been enamored of figure skating and the incredible feats these athletes perform on thin blades of steel. I was fortunate to have the opportunity to interview Elena Berezhnaya, Olympic gold medalist at the 2002 Winter Games for pairs figure skating, while she was in Toronto to perform for Stars on Ice. Despite her youth, Elena's story not only reflects success but is a fantastic example of both maturity and serial bounce-back.

She grew up in an area called Nevinnomirsk near the Black Sea in Russia. When she was four years old, like many Russian children she and her brother were brought to the new ice rink in her hometown to try out for skating lessons. Her mother couldn't find skates to fit her small feet, so Elena had to use a pair that were enormous for her. That didn't take away from her obvious ability, though, and she went on to train with a coach full time.

At twelve, her coach took her to Moscow to start training in pairs. She skyrocketed to success and, after skating together for two years, fifteen-year-old Elena and her partner Oleg Sliakhov became the first pair to compete in the World Championships for Latvia in 1993. They finished fourteenth at the Worlds, and showed more promise when they placed eighth at the Lillehammer Olympics and seventh at the World Championships the following year. The team was quickly becoming well known in the skating community for their speed, power, and impressive tricks.

Although Elena and her partner were enjoying great success, they hid a dark secret. For years, she had been enduring physical abuse from Oleg. The young, frightened Elena didn't speak with anyone about the abuse, not even her mother. But in 1996, while they were practicing side-by-side camel spins, Oleg's skate blade sliced Elena's head. The exact details of this incident are different, depending on who's telling the story, but the outcome is consistent. Elena was rushed to the hospital and underwent two surgeries to remove pieces of bone from her brain. Miraculously, she recovered and was back on the ice within a few months. "I think the people around me were more scared than I was," she says. "For me, it felt as if I was relearning to walk."

For a young athlete, this kind of emotional and physical trauma could have been devastating. But Elena focused on the bounce-back. During this entire crisis, she and fellow skater Anton Sikharulidze became close friends and, less than a year after Elena's near-fatal injury, the pair entered their first competition together. In December 1997 they placed second at the Russian Nationals, and after further successes Elena was considered one of the best skaters in Europe—just one year after her accident.

You'd think that a near-fatal accident would be enough of a setback for a young athlete, but Elena faced another potential barrier to success. In 2000, she and Anton, two-time world champions and the 1998 Olympic silver medalists, had to withdraw from the 2000 World Figure Skating Championships when Elena tested positive for a banned stimulant that was in an over-the-counter medication she had been advised to take for bronchitis.

"I cried for one week," she said. "And then I remembered that I'm part of a team—with Anton and my coach—and I focused on moving forward as a team. So we asked ourselves the tough questions: Do we want to keep skating? Do we want to skate together? Do we want to win? When it was clear that all our answers were yes, we decided to only look forward and not look back."

As this beautiful, diminutive athlete explained her philosophy of life, I was struck by what I saw—an ambitionist with maturity. The American statesman Bernard M. Baruch once observed that "the art of living lies not in eliminating but in growing with troubles." Elena, by youthful example, reminds us that serial bounce-back isn't necessarily an acquired skill but rather something that you can choose to embrace.

Building Character

What scares people about the notion of maturity is that ambition will wane, pale, and dry up over time. In fact, the opposite is true. By focusing on serial bounce-back, mature ambitionists are forced to design their ambition so that it accommodates not just their vocational aspirations but all aspects of their lives. This adds another challenge to the maturity equation, but it also adds a renewed sense of energy and drive.

> **What scares people about the notion of maturity is that ambition will wane, pale, and dry up over time. In fact, the opposite is true.**

Wayne Scott explains: "When you're twenty, if you want to make money everything you have to do is applied to this one goal. But at forty, you might define success differently—you might want to evolve culturally, learn new skills, find ways to give back to the community, redefine your business. This is simply a mature approach to incorporating one's life experiences and reflecting them in the decisions you make. By applying a richer set of values, you can rely on the fact that ambition is a constant, but you're accommodating the fact that it will show up in different ways and challenge you every time."

The French philosopher Henri Bergson said, "To exist is to change, to change is to mature, to mature is to go on creating oneself endlessly." Whether you're challenged by difficult decisions, honestly assessing your skills, or recommitting to curiosity, the ultimate benefit of maturity is the strength of character it affords you when taking a step toward your ambitious goals. To benchmark successful character building, you can think of maturity as encompassing five challenges: fear, choice, responsibility, power, and performance.

FEAR

We all have fears that relate to our ambition. Some people fear failure and the setbacks it entails, while others are more afraid of success and the changes it will bring on. Yet fear is necessary in order to succeed because it provides a boundary—something to push against. And naming your fear out loud is one of the best ways to reduce its potency. Chan Han Goh speaks openly of the inevitable end of her career as a principal dancer. Bob Faulkner identifies his own "lack of youth and athletic ability" as an adventure racer. Chan and Bob not only reflect a mature stance in relation to their biggest fears; they're building their strength of character on them.

CHOICE

Once you've faced your greatest fear in the realm of ambition, the next step is embracing choice, or what's often termed "being at choice." By allowing failure to define who you are, you're choosing to succumb to it. But by allowing it to be something you gain experience from, you're choosing to find ways to work around it and to focus on what it teaches you. Strength of character, in other words, comes from setting your course of action rather than falling victim to circumstances.

RESPONSIBILITY

Be careful what you wish for, as the saying goes, because you just might get it. After all, with choice comes responsibility—toward the people you hire, the business you generate, the risks you take, and the effects that all these will have on your personal world. And the integrated cycle of ambition means that you need to keep cycling through the various ways of slicing up your pie, making adjustments that are accountable. Dr. Susan Lieberman made the decision to translate her interest in the environment to the realm of policy and politics. In doing so, she accepted the responsibility that goes along with breaking new ground (the CITES policies she was spearheading), as well as the potential effect her decision might have on family and friends who still thought she should be an academic or a doctor. Though her focus was on sustaining her interest and pursuing her curiosity, her steadfastness reflected a character that was strengthening alongside her vocational milestones.

POWER

Many people mistakenly assume that with failure comes a loss of power. *True* power, however, comes from the ability to reinvent success after failure. I devoted a whole chapter of my first book to women and entrepreneurship, and, not surprisingly, the discomfort many women have with power—their own and that of others. Susie Maloney—a Winnipeg-based, best-selling author hailed as the next Stephen King when her second book, the 1998 horror novel titled *A Dry Spell*, garnered a million-dollar deal with Tom Cruise's production company—talks about power in the context of ambition. "Power is incredibly sexy. But in many ways, unfamiliar territory for a lot of women." I could not agree with her more. For Susie, power translated into knowing when to quit dead-end jobs and pursue a girlhood dream of writing "the best damn horror novels ever written." She experiences ambition as a way of empowering herself to change her circumstances.

> **Honestly acknowledging the role of power within the ambitious journey is not only a sign of maturity but also a sign of strength of character.**

Male or female, mature ambitionists recognize their power as part of their realistic self-inventory. They use it responsibly—in the choices they make, in overcoming their fears, and in regaining momentum after a major setback. Honestly acknowledging the role of power within the ambitious journey is not only a sign of maturity but also a sign of strength of character.

PERFORMANCE

Ultimately, strength of character is reflected in your actions and behavior, not your thoughts. And that's why performance is such an important concept in the context of bounce-back and maturity. One way to look at the performance aspect of maturity came to me while reading a fascinating book called *Bobos in Paradise* by David

Brooks. In his work of "comic sociology," Brooks describes the hybrid lifestyle of the urban upper class, with its combination of bohemian values and bourgeois sensibility.

"Companies are trying to cultivate in their employees a faculty that in classical times was known as *metis* . . . ," he writes. "We might call it practical knowledge, cunning, or having a knack for something. . . . The person who acquires metis must learn by doing, not by reasoning and dreaming. . . . For example, an apprentice may learn the rules of cooking, but only a master chef will have the awareness to know when the rules should be applied and when they should be bent or broken."

Similarly, it's only through the benefit of their own hands-on experience—the successes and the inevitable failures—that ambitionists are able to attain not only mastery of their vocation but maturity in their actions.

The transition from the balance to the maturity stage is marked by your strength of character—by admitting to fear, embracing choice, living with responsibility, acknowledging the role of power, and ultimately reflecting character in your actions. Whereas the ambitionist in the balance stage determined what to sacrifice, the mature ambitionist monitors and adjusts the ratios among the elements of the entire cycle. And so, in the ever-changing dynamic nature of ambition, one's character is already being formed.

A FINAL WORD

Maturity demands reflection and careful assessment. But it also represents the necessary pause that allows ambitionists to take stock of the skills they've collected throughout the earlier five stages of ambition and, in preparation for the seventh and last rule of the ambitious journey, to carefully determine what they value most.

But part of taking a pause is simply that: an isolated moment that allows you to look around and take it all in before moving on. Having gained strength of character, mature ambitionists have also cultivated the ability to stop and smell the roses, to truly engage in the present as they career towards the future.

Bob Faulkner recounts just such a moment: "I was in Alaska on one particular race. It was 3:00 a.m. and I was pulling a sled by myself along the Yentna River. Everything was frozen solid, it was forty degrees below zero, and there wasn't a soul in sight. I looked up and saw the Northern Lights, like you've never before seen. And despite the intensity of the plunging temperature, I'm thinking this is pretty fantastic and as good as it gets.

"Then I looked ahead, and out of nowhere I saw a light coming towards me. At first I thought I was imagining it, but I kept staring ahead and the light got closer and closer. Finally I realized it was a dogsled team, so I got off the trail because in Alaska there's an unwritten rule that the dogsleds rule the trails. As I stood to the side of the river, I watched this huge dogsled team sweep by—not making a sound as they mushed—and there was this woman by herself, heading the team. We were fifty miles from nowhere. As she passed we both said hi and she moved on.

"To me, the combination of the beauty of the moment with the sight of this lone woman with a dogsled team racing through Alaska at three in the morning is one of the reasons I do adventure racing. . . . It reminds me of the beauty, the surprise, and the delight of the adventures you bump into. And that makes it all worthwhile."

RULE 7

BELIEF

To accomplish great things, we must not only act,
but also dream; not only plan, but also believe.
—Anatole France

I have this memory. It's right after university, and I'm preparing for my first important job interview. I'm talking to a human resources consultant, who happens to be a friend of the family, and trying to soak up as much information and tricks of the trade as possible. Out of everything he said, I distinctly remember his telling me, "When they ask you a question and are soliciting your opinion about a process, an idea, or an approach, never use terms like 'I believe' or 'I feel' because that comes across as too involved, too subjective. You want to come across as completely objective in your answers—because, after all, that's what a potential boss will be looking for."

I took his advice, and I got the job. But over the years—as I moved up the vocational ladder, running my own business and then coaching others through writing and speaking—I've come to recognize the folly in his approach. Yes, it's true that objectivity and a cool head are crucial to making business decisions. But ultimately, the words that follow "I believe . . ." are what your peers, employees, customers, and partners will remember. More important, it's only by focusing on and testing your beliefs that you're able to create a vision for your own lifework that has lasting meaning.

RE-EVALUATING YOUR JOURNEY

Like any final stage in a cycle, Rule 7 marks both an amalgamation of the preceding stages and a jumping-off point for beginning the cycle again. Rule 7 is all about recognizing the criteria for assessing your belief system, re-evaluating your journey to date, and finding ways to renew your ambition that will propel you into a new round of discovery.

Achieving these three objectives is a tall order. As I searched for ways to help you navigate through these ideas, I looked for patterns and strategies that worked for those I interviewed, in my own experience, and in the research I've conducted over the years. Though the scope of belief goes far beyond the confines of this one chapter, here are the six strategies to consider.

Aligning head, heart, body, and soul These elements contribute to the way in which you think, feel, act upon, and contemplate ideas. Ambitionists recognize the four elements at play and then, when decision making, focus on ways to balance the most challenging alignment: the head versus the heart.

Updating your values The question of values arises, of course, throughout the previous six rules of ambition. In this final stage, the focus is not so much on questioning your values as on determining which of them have changed—and ensuring that you've incorporated this evolution into your definition of success.

Determining if you have a calling Some ambitionists feel a strong sense of obligation to a certain cause, profession, or goal. Discovering if this is how you view your work and your life ambitions will set a course that's different from those of us who do not. And with it comes a level of responsibility that will affect how you evaluate belief and how you will evolve your ambition the next time around.

Reinventing yourself Rather than waiting for whatever changes come their way, ambitionists proactively look for ways to reinvent themselves, whether that means a small adjustment to a vocational goal or a radical shift into new territory altogether. Either way, the very act of personal reinvention will allow you to re-evaluate your journey to date and renew commitment to your values.

Allowing for unpredictability As with anything as elusive as ambition, there's always an element of the unknown. Ambitionists know that the unforeseen will, in one way or another, play a role in the decisions they make and the beliefs they recommit to.

Leaving a legacy When you design your own ambition, you take your drive and momentum and mold it into something lasting that can be passed on to others. Regardless of whether you have a calling and whether you commit to altruistic activities, the true ambitionist works toward leaving a legacy.

Aligning Head, Heart, Body, and Soul

There's always someone ready to throw out one of a host of maddening platitudes aimed at keeping us on our toes—"attain happiness," "find balance," "be fulfilled," "focus on creativity," "stay strategic" . . . the list goes on. Among these unattainable goals is the notion of being able to align your head, heart, body, and soul in the work you choose to do. And yet, after reviewing each and every interview conducted for this book, I recognized a pattern: it's in the pursuit of this elusive goal that success is achieved. Rather than focusing on whether or not they were able to align the four elements, the very act of recognizing their importance became these ambitionists' catalyst for achievement.

Head By applying our intellect and analytical skills we gain objectivity in decision making. Yet without the balance of the other three elements, analytical strength can become lopsided in its pursuit of the straight and narrow. Rather than committing to rationality as the only criterion for thoughtful decisions, remember that the momentum and power of the heart move it forward.

Heart At the other end of the spectrum is heart, the very pulse of ambition. The momentum that comes from desire is what triggers intuition and nuance, which are so crucial in engaging others and making timely decisions. At the same time, heart on its own can draw you into making purely subjective decisions that can sometimes be disastrously irrevocable.

Body There's no doubt that how we care for our bodies affects how we function, not only physically but intellectually and emotionally. Today, the speed with which we are required to perform, decide, change, adapt, and move into action has become so heightened that as much as anything else, it's necessary to be able to handle the physical challenges of keeping up with our own ambition. At the same time, our ambitious pursuits should incorporate our physical need for activity as well as for rest and recovery.

Soul At the end of the day, our decisions and our actions are a reflection of what we believe in. Soul is what tends to be talked about least in the realm of business. And yet it's the reason we put our intellect to work; it's the wellspring of our emotional responses; and it's what moves us to pursue what we value. The most important element of the soul in this context is our beliefs, for they are what will help create our legacies. When Jim Collins, author of *Good to Great: Why Some Companies Make the Leap . . . and Others Don't*, challenges his clients to figure out what they want to be remembered for a hundred years from now, what he's really asking for is a recommitment to their belief system and how well it's reflected in the work they do.

Each of these four elements plays off the others, of course. And depending on the challenges we face and our level of comfort in each area, the significance of each element will shift. Some people naturally prioritize their physical needs above those of the head and heart; others are drawn toward soul searching as a starting point for their endeavors. Regardless of one's inclination, to successfully balance all of these elements all the time is a near impossibility. What *is* important is keeping the dialogue going between them. By staying true to this process, you'll define your own questions of ambition, desire, and success rather than relying on others'.

HEAD-VERSUS-HEART DECISIONS

Throughout the years, when I've challenged any of my clients, interview subjects, or unsuspecting peers with the concept of aligning the head, heart, body, and soul, most people admitted to me that in making decisions and managing their ambition, the struggle between the head and the heart was the most challenging for them. After all, most people care for their bodies as a means of maintaining energy and stamina; and when it comes to the soul, many find that they don't have the time or inclination to focus on such a bigger-than-life theme on a day-to-day basis. What tended instead to draw people's attention was the struggle between what they want emotionally in their lifework and what their intellect told them was required. And although it created the greatest source of potential conflict for them internally, if properly managed, it was also the source of ongoing success and escalating achievements. Ultimately, it reminded them of what their core beliefs are.

Kate Spade is an internationally acclaimed company with sales of approximately $70 million and a few hundred employees. Not only have I admired their handbags and other products, but I've been fascinated with how they conduct themselves in such a cutthroat business. And so I asked Andy Spade, business and life partner of Kate Spade, how he approaches the four elements. This is what he said:

"Physically, I have to take care of myself, just because of the pace of the business—so I make it a point to get out in the fresh air, to leave New York City and make sure my body is happy on a regular basis. Soul? Well, that's such a big unknown that I think each of us constantly struggles with it in our own way, knowing that we always will. So I'd have to say that 'head' is easiest and 'heart' is hardest for me. I'm a very emotional person, so although as a businessperson I know what to do—i.e., my thinking is clear—my heart often struggles with the decision at hand. When we make a decision that's emotionally difficult—like having to let someone go in the company—that lingers with me, as it does for Kate. In the end, though, I'd rather be remembered as an interesting, caring person than a savvy businessperson. And ultimately that's what I take with me when I go to sleep at night."

When we face difficult decisions, we're really dealing with the following question: Should we act from intuition or is it better to be rationally purposeful in our actions? And it's when we bring this question to the table as a partner, a boss, or a leader that they're most challenging. For example, as an employer, do we analyze a person's contribution to the company and determine if we should let him or her go based purely on performance, or should we perhaps find another position for that person because we know intuitively that he or she is hardworking and loyal?

> "I think it's far better to have a philosophy—and others have found this—whereby you can learn to let your brain be your heart's soldier and define places where your heart would be happy."

I once had an assistant who wasn't really fitting into the company culture. I gave her two months to prove herself, after which I came to the conclusion that it wasn't going to work. I sat her down and explained why I felt she had to leave, and offered her a fair severance. To my surprise, she came back to me a few days later, explained why we weren't working well together, and suggested a new process and structure that would be more efficient and enjoyable. I was so impressed with her persistence and courage that I decided to agree to another month to determine if her scheme would pay off. It worked brilliantly. She remained with the company for three years and was the best assistant I ever had. Had I only listened to my head, she would have been let go from the company according to plan. By listening to my intuition I not only kept a good employee but reflected my values in my actions—a combination of head and heart.

The head-heart conflict also comes into play in your individual "happiness quotient." Here's how Po Bronson explains it: "If you only use your brain for making decisions, then very often that will lead you to look for things that will be challenging and stimulating, and you'll ultimately look for lots of activity and 'business.' But in the process you may be denying your heart a certain level of fulfillment and happiness that it craves. I think it's far better to have a philosophy—and others have found this—whereby you can learn to let your brain be your heart's soldier and define places where your heart would be happy. In doing so, you're allowing your ambition to create a place that's far more fulfilling on all fronts."

For Andy Spade, the happiness quotient is at the core of how he and partner Kate do business. Currently, Kate Spade is a well-known label with cachet and a growing following. They're not looking to be the leader in their field, however. "We'd much rather be in the top ten in our industry and be able to conduct our business in a way that reflects our values. We like the fact that we're not number one—it allows us to take the time for the things that are important to us; it allows us to 'strategize our life before we strategize our business,' which means that we listen to our head *and* our hearts, without forfeiting one for the other. And that's what matters to us most."

The happiness quotient, by the way, isn't only a qualitative criterion for doing business; it also affects the bottom line. Many books and studies focus on the head–heart issue, particularly as it relates to motivating employees and the effect this has on their productivity. For example, the Career Innovation Group, an alliance of international blue-chip companies, recently conducted a survey called "Inspiration At Work" that focuses on some of the secrets of non-financial motivation in entrepreneurial startups, NGOs, and charities as part of a project to identify what it takes to be an "inspiring company." This survey was the result of an earlier Gallup survey, which reported that "less than a quarter of workers are fully 'engaged' in their work, costing the US economy $300 billion per year (and £50 billion in the UK)."

"The costs of failing to engage people's hearts and minds are huge. This damages performance whatever the economic climate," commented survey director Charles Jackson. "But in tough times people's commitment is really put to the test. We have found in our initial research that companies with a strong sense of purpose are able to carry people through tough times. Loyalty to a cause, and to colleagues, is still a valuable commodity."

Updating Your Values

In the third, belonging stage of the ambitious journey, ambitionists must define their values as a means of generating a following and engaging others. Now, at the end of the cycle, ambitionists take enough of a pause to ensure that what they originally defined as valuable is still relevant to them.

Performance manager Mackie Shilstone has a pretty straightforward approach: "If you want to figure out how you want to live your life, you need to first ask yourself how you want to die. At first this might sound morbid and dramatic, but it allows you to truly question what you value and then move toward it with speed and accuracy."

So if you decide that you want to die "young old," for example, you may commit to ongoing, high-participation activities and challenges right up until you're no longer physically able. If you're more focused on taking care of yourself and maintaining a certain level of restraint, the work you choose and the endeavors you favor will reflect perhaps less commitment and steer you in the direction of safe bets. Taking a moment to determine how you want to ultimately exit will naturally lead to thoughts about what you truly value. There's really no quicker or more powerful way to make sure that you're not carrying around a set of outdated values. They may, in fact, be the very thing preventing you from moving forward.

Sometimes, updating values is simply an exercise in editing out what no longer works. In his national bestseller *Good to Great,* Jim Collins includes a "Start a 'Stop Doing' List." Those who have built what he refers to as "good-to-great companies" use these lists as a means of getting rid of "extraneous junk" within a corporation. Ambitionists would equally benefit from creating a "stop valuing" list, identifying those values that no longer work for them or no longer reflect what they truly care about.

When Kate and Andy Spade first decided to get into the handbag business, they didn't begin by saying that they wanted to be the best handbag manufacturers around. Instead, "our goal was to have a full, interesting life and we thought that by starting our own company we could reflect that in everything we did." In essence, Andy and Kate looked at what they valued and then went about finding a forum, process, or vessel to contain, communicate, and live those values. This has extended to their company as well. "We believe in graciousness and politesse, and so our designs, our company, and the way we treat our employees all reflect this. Diesel sells hip and Calvin Klein sells sexiness, but that's not what we're about. So we sell graciousness, and we think of people like Grace Kelly and Katharine Hepburn as icons of that image. We demand politesse in our customer service, we reflect these values in our ads, and in the end we've created a world that reflects our own beliefs."

Many people start out with certain beliefs but find that the world they live in or the working environment they have to contend with wears them down and undermines what they uphold as important. Again, the discipline of constantly revisiting your values and updating your work ethic to match it is crucial. Andy and Kate were born in Arizona and Kansas City, respectively, and faced this same challenge when they landed in New York. "When we got here, we realized that either we'd become like everyone around us or we'd try to set a standard of how we wanted to do business and commit to it. There was no choice for us. We knew we could only live with a business that reflected our way of operating. It may not be as savvy and as tough as others, but as Kate says, we need to be able to put our heads on our pillows at night."

Determining If You Have a Calling

If the purpose of the belief stage is to take stock of your values and to realign them with your next set of goals and desires, then at this point it behooves ambitionists to honestly assess if they're one of those who have a true calling. In doing so, it's important not to bring judgment to the table. Instead, focus on the following questions: If I could spend fifteen hours a day doing any one thing, what would it be? Am I motivated by serving others? Can I see myself doing anything else? If not, why? Do I accept the responsibility that comes from the work I've chosen?

I turn in this regard to my interview with Dr. Larry Norton, a renowned medical oncologist at the Memorial Sloan-Kettering Cancer Center in New York and an internationally recognized leader in the treatment of breast cancer. He's a presidential appointee to the National Cancer Advisory Board of the National Cancer Institute and is president of the National Alliance of Breast Cancer Organizations. Most notably, he's identified with an approach to therapy called "dose density," a new and more effective way of using anti-cancer drugs based on a mathematical model he developed with his colleagues. In short, this is a man who has demonstrated unparalleled dedication to his profession. And he's had truly little choice in the matter: it's his calling.

> **"Fundamentally, at a very early age I wanted to do something of lasting value—not transient—whatever that was."**

After the usual protracted arrangements with the hospital's public relations department, I finally found myself seated in Larry Norton's office at Memorial Sloan-Kettering amid medical journals, stacks of papers, charts, and a telephone that never stopped ringing. Larry's story begins as I suspect many doctors' stories do. "I wanted to be a physician very early in the picture. A relative of mine is a vascular surgeon, and I've always been close to him. He was an important influence because he always gave me the reality test against my ideas. Fundamentally, at a very early age I wanted to do something of lasting value—not transient—whatever that was. And frankly, I never remember a time when medicine was not a possibility."

But knowing what you want to do and finding your calling are not one and the same. For Larry, there were two transforming events that led directly to the important work he does today.

The first event took place in second grade. At a public school in the Bronx, he had a substitute art teacher who asked the class to draw the statue of the cowboy she had brought into class. When they finished, she came over to him and said, "Larry, you did such a good job, how about if you now draw it from the other side." He stayed in his seat and drew the statue the way he imagined it would look from the other side. "When I finished, I saw that all my classmates had changed their seats to the other side of the statue. Rather than humiliating me, though, the teacher chose to praise my ability to see the other side of the statue without even getting up and going to the other side of the classroom. It gave me confidence, recognizing that I had an ability to see things visually that others may not have been able to see.

"So now we fast-forward to college. I'm studying organic chemistry, which is a very important course for pre-med students. Like everybody else, I was working very hard to get the best grade possible. And in studying the given textbook for the course I come across this picture of a sugar molecule, showing the various angles. I looked at this complicated molecule and I applied the same visual skill that I had used in grade two and had been perfecting over the years by simply drawing everything from as many different angles as possible—seeing it all in my mind. I immediately knew the diagram was incorrect. I brought it to my professor and explained what I thought was wrong with it. He agreed with me and suggested I write to the textbook publisher. So I did. And several weeks later I got a letter back saying that this textbook had gone through five revisions and generations of grad students and nobody had ever picked up the error. They agreed to correct it in the next edition, and the author suggested he give a lecture at my college. Just having the acknowledgment from these experts was very gratifying to me."

Larry realized that not only did he have a strong desire to do something of lasting value in medicine, but his ability to see things from a different perspective might eventually lead him to some kind of revolutionary discovery. And so it did. Today, his unconventional approach to cancer treatment is based on a mathematical model that came out of his visual abilities. Thousands of people have benefited from his methods, which are purported to cut the annual odds of death from breast cancer by 31 percent. Now that is a calling worth pursuing.

When I asked Larry to describe how he knows that his is a calling and not simply a profession, he related the following story.

"Years ago, I was giving a lecture on breast cancer to a room full of doctors and medical experts in Cincinnati. I looked around and I saw the typical doctors and nurses, but I also noticed two people who didn't look like they belonged. The man was in a suit and you could tell he wasn't comfortable; she was wearing a new dress; their faces were weathered and their hands rough—they just didn't fit. So we finished the morning session and this couple approached me. As it turns out, they were farmers. Three years earlier she'd had a very severe form of breast cancer. She went to the local doctor who suggested she go to a big city to an expert. This was out of the question for them, since she couldn't afford to take the time or money it would require to do this. She simply asked the doctor if he could do the best he could.

"This doctor had recently read a paper I'd written describing a different approach to the disease. Apparently, he had called me and I worked with him extensively by telephone in terms of calculating the doses and working through the mathematical approach that I had devised. This doctor followed my instructions and the woman had a fantastic response, got operated on locally, and got chemo. Three years later she was cured. And when they found out that I was coming to Cincinnati, they drove a hundred miles, registered, and paid for the lecture just so they could tell me how I saved her life. They wanted to personally thank me for changing their lives forever."

As Larry is telling me this story, I'm not the only one with teary eyes. "I mean, when you're faced with moments like that, whether you call it ambition, a calling, belief, or dedication, it really doesn't matter. The whole concept that one can write a paper based on one's work—and yes, it is part of your work, but the fact that you can actually save a life halfway across the country for someone you never met—that kind of impact at a distance is what my life is about. And when you ask me to define ambition, I guess the answer is to make that kind of difference for as many lives as possible for as long as I can."

Reinventing Yourself

For many of us, a calling is not in the cards. Or perhaps it is and, unfortunately, we might never recognize it. But for those of us struggling with defining the work we do in the context of who we are, the important guiding principle is that ambition evolves over time and change is a constant. And by finding ways to renew their beliefs through personal reinvention, ambitionists can bring meaning to what they do.

Let's say you're working for a company that you admire, your responsibilities match your skills, and you're challenged and motivated to do your best. But suddenly the company is sold, the corporate culture alters dramatically, and you no longer feel valued for who you are and what you contribute. Just when you thought you'd found what works, you're forced to re-evaluate your situation, skills, talents, desires, and beliefs.

Many of us choose to roll with these changes for a lot longer than is necessary. But when you avoid taking stock in this way, you fall into what I call "ambitious malaise"—you think you're working toward a goal you desire when in fact you're simply playing an old tape in your head that's no longer relevant.

Sometimes this malaise sets in because you've avoided the necessary exercise of reinventing yourself as a means of renewing your beliefs. You started off wanting fame and now you want stability; you started off wanting to make a lot of money and now you value time; you started off believing you had the leadership skills necessary to run your own company and now you realize that your real strength lies in managing others within a larger organization. Whatever the catalyst, ambitionists simply decide to personally reinvent themselves on a regular basis as a means of keeping their beliefs and abilities in line. Of course, having defined themselves and their work through the first six stages—discovery, focus, belonging, momentum, balance, and maturity—they have a solid

By finding ways to renew their beliefs through personal reinvention, ambitionists can bring meaning to what they do.

training that enables them to make important leaps, if warranted, in this final stage of the cycle.

The process of reinventing oneself isn't always easy and often requires a kick-start. Ambitionists make sure that they're constantly asking themselves, "What do I believe in?" or "What do I value?" at important junctures in their careers or lifework. How you choose to reinvent yourself can be as dramatic as changing industries or as subtle as readjusting your work–life balance to match your renewed values.

For example, I know a marketing executive who was intent on writing a book but needed to make a living to support her family. After going through a number of part-time jobs that left her with little time or energy for writing, she finally realized that she wasn't creating a structure to support her beliefs. As soon as she committed to writing, she found a public relations job that used what she was best at and allowed her three days a week to write. By simply renewing her definition of herself ("I'm no longer a marketing executive, but a public relations freelancer") she was able to free herself of an old set of beliefs and focus on her new values.

ALTRUISM AND RENEWAL

Traditionally, people delve into their careers and then, once retired, put their energies into a worthwhile cause. They often don't have a choice; all their energy has to go toward making a living and what remains is devoted to family and friends. But finding a way to introduce altruistic activities, however small, is a wonderful way to update your values and realign your head, heart, body, and soul without having to completely redefine the work you do. In my research on altruism, I found inspiration and insight in two completely different parts of the world and in two completely different areas of work. I start with Franco Carlotto.

Franco is a six-time winner of Mr. World Fitness. He grew up in a little village in Switzerland called Oberuzwil. As a young boy, he was pretty inactive. When he read about people as varied as Gandhi, Mother Teresa, and Muhammad Ali, Franco was fascinated with the barriers they each had to overcome, not only to succeed but to go on to become heroes for others. Then and there, he made a commitment to himself that one day he too would be a hero and inspire others.

> "You really need three things—heart, passion, and faith. I always start with heart—because if you're not working from a place of love, then your work becomes meaningless."

At the age of ten he discovered fitness and soon set his sights on becoming a world champion. But the more involved he became, the more aware he was of a world that focused on muscle building through steroids and other drugs. He decided that he wouldn't succumb to any unnatural aids, and would become a champion based only on his own efforts. And that theme has been at the heart of his work ever since.

Franco won Junior Mr. Fitness for the first time at the age of seventeen, going on to win the championship title six times in a row. But he also made it a priority to teach his ideas about health and fitness to those in need. Today, Franco also runs Fitness for Kids, a nonprofit organization dedicated to teaching and inspiring young people to achieve their highest potential through health and fitness by eating well, staying active, and fostering a positive mental attitude. His organization provides educational and inspirational programs around the world for schools, families, and teachers to help reduce obesity in children and encourage health and activity in teens. Whether he's speaking at an elementary school in Switzerland or conducting an interview on CNN to promote the ideas behind his program, he's dedicated to helping others achieve their highest potential through the metaphor of health and fitness.

Franco is clear about his goals, but he's also very aware of how his altruism constantly renews his own belief system. "A lot of people in my position would look for ways to make money through infomercials and other product promotions. I've been approached many times, and despite the fact that sometimes I was tempted by the potential financial gain, I refused to go down that road. What would it leave me with ultimately? Nothing. Whereas, doing the work I do, I'm living my ultimate dream and my original ambition, which was to be a hero for others and inspire millions of people around the world."

When I asked Franco what he thinks is required to turn raw ambition into something meaningful, his answer was simple: "You really need three things—heart, passion, and faith. I always start with heart—because if you're not working from a place of love, then your work becomes meaningless. It's what sets your ideals in the first place. Secondly, passion. Without passion, it's hard to get the energy to keep going. And lastly, faith—you need to believe in what you're doing. Without this, your ambition might be strong, but it's empty."

Personal reinvention sometimes comes from a place of need and then flourishes into a whole new world of meaning. Lynne Franks—who in the '80s and '90s headed up the largest consumer PR company in the UK—is a great case in point. When I spoke with her in Majorca, Spain, her insights into renewal and reinvention really struck a chord.

Lynne grew up in London and left school at the age of sixteen. She always wanted to be a journalist and, as she describes it, the easiest way to become one was to work as a secretary. So she went to work for a teen magazine and started doing bits of journalism along the way. When she couldn't get the journalism job she wanted, she went to work for a public relations firm for a few years. At that time public relations was a new industry, and by age twenty-one she had enough experience dealing with the press and working on PR campaigns that she felt ready to start her own business.

Like many self-starters, Lynne began by working from her home. Her first client was Katharine Hamnett, who was one of the first artists to use slogans on T-shirts as a means of communicating political statements. Lynne gained ground through this campaign and quickly began picking up other clients in design, fashion, music, and pop culture. Over twenty years she built up a team of fifty people and became an icon in the industry, often cited as the guru of lifestyle public relations in the UK. Her work extended from creating and running London Fashion Week (a biannual international event showcasing ready-to-wear designer fashions) to promoting campaigns for organizations like Amnesty, Greenpeace, and Fashion Cares/AIDS Awareness.

In short, Lynne and her company were legendary. But in 1992 it all changed. After twenty years of juggling it all—wife, mother of two, industry icon—Lynne sold her business. In the process, the structure and beliefs that had kept her going for so many years fell apart around her—her health started to fail, her marriage collapsed—and she quickly realized that a reinvention was absolutely necessary.

She turned her attention to a number of volunteer committees and causes, and soon found herself drawn to issues that revolved around women and work. Since she had experienced such success in the fashion and pop culture world, she'd rarely felt at a disadvantage being a woman. But when she got out into the "real" world, she was shocked to discover the many barriers women had to overcome in work and in life, and she wanted to help change that. In 1995, in anticipation of the UN Beijing Women's Conference to be held later that year, Lynne organized a high-profile event in England called What Women Want. Not only was the event extremely successful in its own right, but Lynne, with her public relations skills in hand, was able to pique the interest of journalists worldwide and gain coverage on women's issues that had long been avoided. This was the beginning of her renewal.

"I began traveling all over the world, lecturing at events and, in particular, speaking to women who had changed their lives and made changes—women in Africa, Asia, etc. In the process I realized that I'd been so cocooned in a public relations world that revolved around materialism and consumerism. Suddenly, I was dealing with issues that really mattered to me. It was life changing."

> **"Though I always participated in nonprofit endeavors, even at the peak of my PR days, today I've found a way to relate my values to my work directly—and that makes all the difference."**

Today Lynne is the author of several books, including *The Seed Handbook* and *Grow: The Modern Women's Handbook*. She runs SEED, an organization dedicated to educating and inspiring women around the world to become financially empowered. "I gained fulfillment in my life, which was so radically absent. Though I always participated in nonprofit endeavors, even at the peak of my PR days, today I've found a way to relate my values to my work directly—and that makes all the difference."

There are many instances of those who have come to focus on altruistic activities. Hollywood celebrities such as Paul Newman, for example, have devoted themselves to making a difference. After Newman's son Scott died of a drug overdose, he and his wife, Joanne Woodward, began the Scott Newman Foundation, which is dedicated to educating people about drug and alcohol abuse. His food line, called Newman's Own, produces everything from healthy salad dressings to spaghetti sauce, and he donates a good portion of his profits to charities in the arts, children's causes, disaster relief, environmental causes, and hunger relief. Based on the $80 million he raised for various charities, in 1994 Newman received the Jean Hersholt Humanitarian Award. "There's nothing exceptional or noble in being philanthropic," he once said. "It's the other attitude that confuses me."

Paul Newman, among others, is a tough role model to emulate. But altruistic work can happen in many ways and take many forms. What matters most is the decision to integrate it into your life.

Jamie Oliver is a case in point. At twenty-eight, he's already a famous chef, best-selling cookbook author, and winning TV personality. But what's he spending a lot of his time on now? A nonprofit restaurant that puts his culinary talents toward a good cause. Working with a charity called Cheeky Chops, Oliver trains fifteen unemployed youth with little or no cooking experience at his new restaurant in London, aptly named Fifteen. The goal is to allow underprivileged, budding cooks to get a head start. Fifteen isn't profitable yet, but it's been receiving rave reviews since it opened in the fall of 2002—and getting a table can often mean waiting for several weeks, if not months. The venture is Oliver's way of giving back to his profession, and like any restaurant, it's not always easy. But despite the unavoidable stresses, Oliver has stepped into the role of mentor with enthusiasm: "I've learned a lot about people. They're all individuals. Each learns and reacts in his or her own way. . . . You have to be patient and firm." For those ready to incorporate altruistic activities into their ambitious journey, here are a few tactics worth considering:

DON'T WAIT TO GIVE BACK Franco Carlotto believes it's important to give back to your community, industry, or cause while you're on your way up rather than waiting until you're older, supposedly wiser, and have more time. "There's nothing more empowering than giving back. It inspires you to give more and more each time, and in the process not only are you helping someone else, but you're renewing your own sense of success at a very personal level."

This mimics what Chan Hon Goh decided to do in writing her autobiography. She wanted young girls reading the book to be able to relate to a dancer at the height of her career—knowing that that immediacy would make all the difference. It also reinforces what Jerry Mitchell talked about in choreographing shows to raise money for AIDS at his very busiest time in his career.

FIND THE FORUM THAT WORKS Some people simply want to give money. Others want to be involved in the very act of giving—whether handing out food in a shelter or delivering gifts to needy children at Christmas. Some people need to create their own organization and control the means by which they distribute, educate, inspire, and assist. Others find that their time limitations oblige them to choose an organization they respect and simply slot themselves into an area where they can make the best contribution. The message is simple: do what reflects your own values, join a cause that you truly care about, and find a forum that will maximize your time and abilities.

TALLY YOUR TALENTS Some people get frustrated in their altruistic endeavors because they feel that sitting through long, drawn-out board meetings or participating in committees that aren't always efficient is a waste of time and energy. And so, regardless of the endeavor you choose, be honest with yourself and others about your strengths. Agree to do only what you know you can do easily and with professionalism. It will inspire both you and others and get the job done for those who need it most.

LOOK AT THE BIG PICTURE For those who are thinking of dedicating their career to an altruistic cause, Lynne Franks's books are an excellent guide to what's involved in this process. One of her principles is to look at the big picture—not just what you want do to, but where you want to live, how you want to spend your time and money, and how you see yourself evolving over the years. Often, she says, people stumble into a line of altruistic work, get excited by it, and then a few years later are disappointed by the way it has inadvertently changed their lifestyle. Although it may be tempting to be swept away by the virtue of a cause, make sure to do your own spiritual audit before committing your time

> **As tempting as it is to provide a set roadmap for belief, the truth is that journeys meander, change is inevitable, and the element of surprise is unavoidable.**

and energy. Lynne also reminds us to take heed of a Catalan saying, *"A poc a poc"*: step by step.

Allowing for Unpredictability

As tempting as it is to provide a set roadmap for belief, the truth is that journeys meander, change is inevitable, and the element of surprise is unavoidable. Regardless of how you decide to reinvent yourself and assess your beliefs, you must always leave room for a certain element of unpredictability.

When I speak to audiences around the world, I always try to find a way to cite the literary term "magic realism" as a means of reminding careerists and entrepreneurs alike that success often comes through a combination of serendipity and pragmatism. If you're all about the bottom line, or seeing the world in black and white, you might not have the imagination to recognize opportunities when they're right in front of you. Conversely, while you may be dreaming and scheming, at a certain point, it's those who can keep their feet firmly planted on the ground who ultimately are able to win the race.

Andy Spade describes the important role that unpredictability played in his ambitious journey. After building up the company for a few years, he felt that he simply could not make one more handbag. "I think I was simply getting worn down by the operational issues I had to deal with every day," he says. So what did he do? Despite the company's growing success, he allowed himself to daydream about a new kind of retail venture. He had always been fascinated with merchandise from hardware and hobby stores, and so he began designing a store that featured an array of the unique merchandise for men that he loved best, from hardware gadgets to fashion accessories. After a lot of hard work, Andy opened up Jack Spade and received rave reviews.

"I love the fact that I'm able to integrate a lending library and a used bike store. I mean, who thinks of a handbag manufacturer and then thinks of a lending library? Creating this surprising store really liberated me. It gave me a chance to look at everything we did at Kate Spade in a new light—from the store design to the advertising to the day-to-day operation. It was the perfect way to renew my belief in the intuitive side of business. And in the process, it reminded me of what was really important."

Whether they refer to it as intuition, surprise, unpredictability, or sheer "unknowableness," its importance in the belief stage of ambition has been invoked by everyone I've counseled, interviewed, or spoken with over the years. But it wasn't until I had the pleasure of meeting Rita Rogers, one of the most renowned clairvoyants in the UK, that the power of intuition really hit home.

Rita writes a column for *Bella* magazine, was the psychic of Diana, Princess of Wales, has been on every talk show worldwide from CNN's *Larry King Live* to *Good Morning America*, and is the author of several best-selling books on spirituality. And after interviewing her in London, I wasn't surprised by her list of accomplishments and her admirers in an industry that's often viewed with cynicism and fear. Rita's ability to tap into what people are telling her, pick up what they're distinctly avoiding, and communicate it with clarity is uncanny.

Rita is descended from a long line of Romany Gypsies. Born in Scotland, she was the only girl among fourteen children. At the age of ten her grandmother told her that she had the ability to "see," and took her under her wing. Rita was twenty when her grandmother passed on, and she took on the role of the seer in the family. It was meant to be.

During our interview Rita recounted many fascinating stories that reflected how important intuition is to her and how rarely people allow their intuitive self to guide them when they're at a crossroads. But of all her stories, this is the one that struck me most.

A number of years back, Rita received a call from an army general who asked for her assistance in finding two men lost in the Alps on a secret military mission. Having tried every other available high-tech communications device and having wasted six valuable hours, he reluctantly came to her, based on the advice of one of his men who had heard of her famous intuitive powers. Within minutes, Rita knew the exact location of these men and described it with accuracy. But this didn't sit right with the general, and he couldn't bring himself to deploy a helicopter based on one woman's vision. Rita begged him to find the men before midnight, which she knew was the longest they could hold out.

Finally, a helicopter was sent around 2 a.m. The location was spot on. Both men were dead. The next day the general called Rita and said, "If only you could have provided me with some logic, some explanation for what you did, I would have acted sooner and avoided this disaster." To which Rita replied, "If only you had allowed yourself a little bit of human intuition or unpredictability, we could have worked together to save those men."

Finding ways to incorporate unpredictability as a means of concluding the journey can be encouraged, but not taught. Ambitionists know this. In fact, they depend on it.

It's no coincidence that as ambitionists move through the seven rules, the free-flowing state of mind required in the first stage, discovery, is once again at play in this last stage. Like all cycles, in completing Rule 7 you return to the beginning of the process and discover ambition anew. Finding ways to incorporate unpredictability as a means of concluding the journey can be encouraged, but not taught. Ambitionists know this. In fact, they depend on it.

Leaving a Legacy

When I asked Dr. Larry Norton how he defined his role—scientist, doctor, or inventor—he replied, "Most important, I'm a teacher." In his world, lasting value is created only by passing on a legacy to the next generation of doctors and scientists who will continue to research and teach. It's a simple formula. As Larry spoke of legacy, however, I was struck by the fact that ambition is often considered self-serving, centered on one's own needs and desires. But by aspiring to create something that will be remembered, revered, read, seen, or talked about, you're really creating the perfect platform for passing on the baton. This also has the effect of liberating ambitionists to move on to other pursuits, knowing that their original efforts will benefit others.

"One of the great moments for me in life was when I was a junior faculty member at Mount Sinai Hospital and I was attending on the ward," Larry continues. "I remember coming in one day to learn that a patient the night before had gone into septic shock, which can be very serious. The intern on call had done all the right things and the patient was fine by the time I arrived the next morning. I couldn't believe that I hadn't been called—I mean, generally the intern is supposed to call the attending physician. When I approached this intern, I said, 'You did a great job and happily everything worked out. But I'm curious, why didn't you call me?' And he said, 'Well, we had a case just like this last week and you very diligently explained to all of us how to treat this situation, so faced with this, I just did it.' It was one of the greatest moments of my career because I was able to not only save someone's life based on my own expertise, but I had passed on the knowledge. I had a great sense of euphoria in knowing that I had contributed in real time to a lasting value."

Franco Carlotto also talks about passing on learning. Once, when he was signing autographs at an elementary school in Atlanta, he was approached by a boy about five years old. The little boy came up to Franco and asked if he could hug him. He then whispered in his ear: "Thank you, Mr. Fitness, for telling me how to be healthy. I'll never forget it." The thrill that Franco got from this encounter far outweighed his excitement at having won one of his many championship trophies.

Whether it's the values we pass on to our children by example, the individuals we influence by our work, or the people we teach face to face, leaving a legacy is at the heart of ambition and sets the stage for our next ambitious journey.

A FINAL WORD

The evolution from raw to managed ambition requires a mindfulness about your belief system—who you are, your goals and values, and a continual redefinition of how you're going to achieve them in a manner that's true to your sense of success.

I always think of university exams when I think of ambition. There are those who are so focused on getting a good mark that all their efforts, all their strategizing revolves around that final outcome. And then there are those who somehow, despite their youth, recognize that there's merit in learning and lasting value in gaining knowledge for knowledge's sake, regardless of the outside world's stamp of approval. And that is a worthwhile pursuit. The same goes for ambition—it's only worth what you gain through the process of understanding it, growing with it, learning from it, and constantly re-evaluating what it means in the context of your world. Getting a good job or gaining recognition is wonderful, fun, and motivating, but it's secondary to the internal dialogue that allows ambitionists to move on.

Larry Norton told me that someone once asked him what he'll do when and if cancer is finally cured. "I'll probably take a week off, go skiing, and then come back and rediscover what it is I need to dedicate my life to curing next . . . and that is the truth."

Alexander the Great is said to have wept because he had no more worlds to conquer. Ambitionists stop pursuing goals only when they no longer recognize the values and beliefs behind their actions. And knowing that it's a never-ending search is what allows the ambitionist to happily return to the first cycle again and again, rediscovering what is new and venturing forward.

EPILOGUE
Getting There

> Make voyages. Attempt them. There's nothing else.
> —*Tennessee Williams*

My original idea for an epilogue was to collect answers to, say, ten burning questions about where our relationship to ambition might be headed. But, interestingly, many of the futurists I approached were reticent about responding to such questions, and, upon reflection, I found this made sense. There is no beginning, middle, or end to ambition as it relates to each of us. Instead it's an ongoing process, a journey that by its nature illuminates our beliefs and values as we redefine it in every stage of our lives. It's a struggle we resent because of what it forces us to sacrifice and grapple with every day, and cherish because of what it teaches us.

And so, rather than try to neatly wrap up the seven rules for getting there and summarize where we're heading, it seemed more relevant to try to define what "getting there" actually might mean. As it turned out, I found the answers in three completely unrelated places.

In 2003 I conducted an online survey at the Girls Intelligence Agency, a California-based company that does research and marketing for companies targeting the female youth market. My intention was simply to get a sense of what young women think about ambition. When asked, "What does ambition mean to you?" 41 percent responded, "Wanting to do whatever it takes to be successful." Yet when asked, "What is most important to you?" 62 percent answered, "A happy life." At the beginning of this book I contrasted the old-world view of ambition—the cutthroat, do-it-at-any-cost definition of success—with today's growing desire to redefine ambition as a positive catalyst for life and vocational fulfillment. Funny that a significant number of the young female respondents to this survey would do whatever it takes to succeed while wanting happiness above all else. Perhaps they understand the concept of "at all costs," not as a conflicted starting point, but as part and parcel of happiness itself. In other words, for this generation, maybe "getting there" will mean their ability to do whatever it takes to create a happy life.

When asked, "Are you more or less ambitious than your girl-friends?" 92 percent said more, and when asked, "Do you see ambition as a positive quality to have?" 98 percent said yes. Do these young respondents not see their friends as ambitious, or do they see themselves as *so* ambitious that others pale in comparison? Either way, there doesn't seem to be much discussion about the fact that to be ambitious is the only choice—and maybe, just by recognizing that it is a choice, they've already begun the journey to getting there.

Finally, when asked, "Who is your role model for an ambitious woman?" more than half the respondents said their mother. In our own struggles with ambition, then, what desires and beliefs are we, as parents, passing on to our children?

My second source of inspiration for the meaning of "getting there" came to me in David Brooks's *Bobos in Paradise*. I kept returning to a particular paragraph. In his description of the ongoing conflict between bourgeois and bohemian values as reflected in the new upper class today, he writes: "But the biggest tension, to put it in the grandest terms, is between worldly success and inner virtue. How do you move ahead in life without letting ambition wither your soul? How do you accumulate the resources you need to do the things you want without becoming a slave to material things? How do you build a comfortable and stable life for your family without getting bogged down in stultifying routine? How do you live at the top of society without becoming an insufferable snob?"

When I thought about it, so many of these very questions formed the conversations and subtext of the interviews I was conducting around the world to help me write this book. And instead of coming up with any answers, each interview became a forum for posing more questions. Such conflicts, it would seem, are universal challenges. No doubt they will continue to plague all of us to varying degrees in the future. What did become clear, however, was that the ambitionist doesn't focus on the futility of reconciling any one of these, but rather chooses a path that accommodates the elements necessary to move from raw ambition to the learning, inquiring, and evolving that translate into managed ambition. And that in itself is a starting point.

> **The ambitionist chooses a path that accommodates the elements necessary to move from raw ambition to the learning, inquiring, and evolving that translate into managed ambition. And that in itself is a starting point.**

But what's at the heart of the ambitionist's approach to this ongoing challenge? My third inspiration came to me in John Steinbeck's *East of Eden*. Halfway through the novel two of the main characters are discussing their views of the New and Old Testaments and the significance of various interpretations. "The King James translation makes a promise in 'Thou shalt,' meaning that men will surely triumph over sin. But the Hebrew word, the word *timshel*—'Thou mayest'—that gives a choice. It might be the most important word in the world. That says the way is open."

This passage reminded me that as a way to conclude my first book, *Bulldog*, I had turned to the Hebrew term *Ein Breira*—which, roughly translated, means "It's unavoidable." It was a good way to describe how, by pushing the boundaries of possibility, new entrepreneurs would inevitably pass on their learning.

Ambition, I realized, called for just the converse: choice. You choose, after all, how far you'll go with your ambition, how far you're willing to push the boundaries, and how many times you'll redefine success for yourself. The ambitionist's mantra, then, might just be *Timshel*—"Thou mayest." It evokes the necessary optimism for defining "getting there" and allows each of us to celebrate the possible on our own terms. And there lies the future of ambition.

NOTES

INTRODUCTION: A WINNING AMBITIONIST APPROACH

p. xi and elsewhere   *appetite, ardor, aspiration, avidity* . . . Synonyms of *ambition*, from *Roget's 21st Century Thesaurus in Dictionary Form*.

p. xiii   **A 1998 Statistics Canada General Social Survey** . . . *The Daily*, Statistics Canada press release on General Social Survey: Time Use, November 9, 1999. Online at www.statcan.ca. The survey interviewed 10,749 people over the age of fifteen who were living in private households across ten provinces. Respondents were asked to report a diary of their time use over a twenty-four hour period.

p. xiv   **"This proportion agrees with studies** . . ." Anna Kemeny, "Driven to Excel: A Portrait of Canada's Workaholics," *Canadian Social Trends*, Spring 2002, Statistics Canada catalogue No. 11-008. Available online at www.statcan.ca/english/indepth/11-008/feature/star200206 4000s1a01.pdf.

p. xiv   **In the US, 78 percent of those questioned** . . . Peter Vogt, *Redefining Career Values*, retrieved October 20, 2003, from http://editorial.careers.msn.com.

RULE 1: DISCOVERY

p. 18   *"instead of judging our way forward* . . ." Edward de Bono, *Six Thinking Hats*. New York: Little, Brown and Back Bay Books, 1999, 3.

Originally published in hardcover in New York by Little, Brown and Company, 1985.

p. 22   *"riding the horse in the direction it's going"*   Linda Obst, *Hello, He Lied—and Other Truths from the Hollywood Trenches*. New York: Broadway Books, 1996, 73.

RULE 3: BELONGING

p. 53   *the importance that Hallmark places on emotional branding* . . . Robinette, Scott and Claire Brand with Vicki Lenz, *Emotion Marketing: The Hallmark Way of Winning Customers for Life*. New York: McGraw-Hill, 2001.

p. 67   *"We had one big advantage when we started our company . . ."* www.katespade.com.

p. 68   *She travels the world extensively* . . . www.designersguild.com.

p. 69   *"For one thing, by treating customers well . . ."* www.katespade.com.

RULE 4: MOMENTUM

p. 86   *"If doing what you love for a living . . ."* *Contract* magazine, January 2002, 34.

p. 99   *"What is the sound of a nation questioning . . ."* Polly LaBarre, "How to Lead a Rich Life," *Fast Company*, March 2003, 72.

p. 99   *the rebirth of Hush Puppy shoes* . . . Malcolm Gladwell, *The Tipping Point: How Little Things Can Make a Big Difference*. New York: Little, Brown and Company—Back Bay Books, 2000, 3–4.

p. 99   *Its makers focused on internet marketing* . . . Mary Elizabeth Williams, "The Blair Witch Project," July 13, 1999. Retrieved October 27, 2003, from www.salon.com.

p. 100   *"What can I say about G-Push . . ."* www.gpush.com

RULE 5: BALANCE

p. 113   *"25 percent of Canadians . . ."* Wallace Immen, "'Role Overload' Makes Workers Sick," *The Globe and Mail*, October 22, 2003, C3.

p. 114 *"almost half of all Canadians . . ."* Conference Board of Canada, "Is Work–Life Balance Still an Issue for Canadians and Their Employers? You Bet It Is!" June 1999.

p. 114 *"80 percent of our medical expenditures . . ."* Melinda Davis, *The New Culture of Desire: 5 Radical New Strategies That Will Change Your Business and Your Life.* New York: The Free Press, 2002, 59.

p. 114 *In Finland, more than 50 percent . . .* "S.O.S. Stress at work: Costs of Workplace Stress Are Rising, with Depression Increasingly Common," *World of Work (Magazine of the International Labour Organization),* No. 37, December 2000.

p. 115 *In the US, clinical depression has become . . .* Ibid.

p. 115 *"The central motivating force of human behavior . . ."* Davis, 76.

p. 115 *a study conducted by the Next Group in the US . . .* Davis, 63.

p. 122 *"How do you get grade twos to be such Picassos . . ."* John Guare, author of play and screenplay for *Six Degrees of Separation,* director Fred Schepisi, 1993.

p. 132 *"you don't just come home with a tan . . ."* Davis, 195–96.

p. 135 *For a fee, there are consultants who specialize . . .* Doug Saunders, "Self-Employed Get Support from Personal Boards, CFOs: Business Directors Provide Work Strategies; 'Woo-Woo Person' Gives Spiritual Guidance," *The Globe and Mail,* September 14, 2002, A3.

p. 136 *"The two things that wealthy people . . ."* Polly LaBarre, "How to Lead a Rich Life," *Fast Company,* March 2003, 79.

RULE 6: MATURITY

p. 156 *"Power is incredibly sexy . . ."* Caroline Nolan, "Ambition," *Scarlett,* May/June 2003, Vol. 1, Issue 1, 27.

p. 157 *"Companies are trying to cultivate . . ."* David Brooks, *Bobos in Paradise: The New Upper Class and How They Got There.* New York: Touchstone, Simon & Schuster, 2000, 131.

RULE 7: BELIEF

p. 167 *"The Career Innovation Group . . ."* Nannette Ripmeester, news release, August 13, 2001. "Creating an Entrepreneurial Culture": a gathering of senior leaders and HR innovators near Paris in November 21, 2001.

p. 168 *"Start a 'Stop Doing' List"* Jim Collins, *Good to Great: Why Some Companies Make the Leap . . . and Others Don't.* New York: HarperBusiness, 2001, 139–140.

p. 180 *"There's nothing exceptional . . ."* Angela Dawson, "Newman's Own Road," Retrieved October 29, 2003, from http://entertainment.sympatico.ca/celebs/features/newman.html.

p. 181 *"I've learned a lot about people . . ."* Marion Kane, "Naked Chef Gives Back," *The Toronto Star,* October 11, 2003, L1–L4. Retrieved October 28, 2003, from www.thestar.com.

EPILOGUE: GETTING THERE

p. 191 *"But the biggest tension . . ."* David Brooks, *Bobos in Paradise: The New Upper Class and How They Got There.* New York: Touchstone, Simon & Schuster, 2000, 41.

p. 192 *"The King James translation makes a promise . . ."* John Steinbeck, *East of Eden.* New York: Penguin Books, 1952, 301.

ACKNOWLEDGMENTS

Writing a book, like so many challenging endeavors, is all about the many people who dedicate themselves to the process.

First and foremost I would like to thank the many readers and audiences that I've had the pleasure of interacting with, and who have taken the time over the last few years to provide me with their issues, questions, and ambitions—which was the original impetus for this book's concept.

I am indebted to each and every one of the high-profile people who agreed to be interviewed for this book—thank you for your honesty, insight, and willingness to explore ambition in all its many facets: Jim Balsillie, chairman and co-CEO of Research In Motion; Cheryl Barker, opera diva; Robyn Benincasa, top female Eco Challenge competitor; Elena Berezhnaya, Olympic gold medalist; Michael Birch, president and owner of The First Nations Buying Group; Po Bronson, best-selling author of *What Should I Do with My Life?;* Hilary Brown, foreign correspondent, ABC News; EJ Camp, celebrity and advertising photographer; Dean Canten, co-founder of international fashion label D-Squared; Franco Carlotto, six-time winner of Mr. World Fitness; Robert

Carsen, world-renowned director; Dr. Clarissa Desjardins, executive vice president, Corporate Development, at Caprion Pharmaceuticals Inc.; Bob Faulkner, oldest Eco Challenge racer; Lynne Franks, author and founder of SEED; Simon Franks, chief executive, Redbus; Chan Hon Goh, principal dancer, the National Ballet of Canada; Tricia Guild, founder, The Designers Guild; Adèle Hurley, senior fellow, Water Issues, Munk Centre, University of Toronto; Silvia Imparato, international vintner, Montevetrano Wines; Eleanor Lambert Berkson, founder of the International Best Dressed Poll; Dr. Susan Lieberman, director, Species Programme, WWF International; Jerry Mitchell, top Broadway choreographer of *Hairspray*, among others; Dr. Larry Norton, head of the division of Solid Tumor Oncology at Memorial Sloan-Kettering Cancer Center; Glenn Pushelberg and George Yabu, founders of Yabu Pushelberg; Karim Rashid, international industrial designer of the Oh Chair, among others; Rita Rogers, UK's top clairvoyant; Wayne Scott, executive coach, Action Strategies Inc.; Mackie Shilstone, performance enhancement expert, Ochsner Clinic Foundation; Andrew J. Spade, co-founder, Kate Spade; Stephen Starr, top restaurateur of Buddakan, among others; Celestina Wainwright Wallis; Andrew D. Watson, director of creation, Cirque du Soleil; Anthony E. Zuiker, creator and executive producer of *CSI* (Crime Scene Investigation).

I could not have completed this book without the hard work and expertise of Robin Kalbfleisch, Kelly O'Neill, and Joy Parker. Thanks also to Lindsay Therrien for her research assistance.

To the professionalism and love of books at the Penguin Canada team—my editor, Susan Folkins, and Karen Alliston, Ed Carson, Andrea Crozier, Debby de Groot, Lesley Horlick, Petra Morin, and Sandra Tooze.

To my literary agents, who are always there for me—Bruce Westwood and Hilary Stanley McMahon and their team at Westwood Creative Artists.

A special thanks to my muse, Gillian Lowe, for her undying ability to generate ideas and motivation at all times.

As always—to Lola for keeping me company, to Lynne for keeping the household running, to my darling Chloë for keeping me buoyant, to my loving husband, Chris, for keeping me focused, and to the memory of my dad, for keeping me inspired.

MAKING CONTACT

I am most interested in your comments and questions regarding ambition. Please forward your queries to **ambition@ellierubin.com** and I would be happy to respond.

For more information on the themes explored in this book as well as a listing of upcoming events, press coverage, and/or booking Ellie Rubin for a speaking engagement, please visit us at **www.ellierubin.com**.

INDEX

ABC (television), 125, 126
Abraham, Dustin Lee, 3
Absenteeism, 114, 115
Accountability, 51, 77–78
Action Strategies Inc., 131
Adams, John, 56–57, 58
Adaptability, 67
Addiction avoidance, 117–26
Addictive personality, 117
Adidas, 52
Adventure racing, 25–27, 39–40, 147–48, 158
Advertising industry, 105
Advice, outside, 37
Agendas, personal. *See* Personal ambitions
Aix-en-Provence Festival, 33
Alienation, avoiding
  full participation, 128–29
  sacrifices, 129–30
  self-reflection, 127–28
Altruism, xvi, 175–81 (*See also* Volunteer work)
  strategies, 181–83
Amazing Technicolor Dream Coat, The, 89
Ambiguity, 20
Ambition
  cycle, xvii
  defining, xii–xiii, xv, 59, 121, 136
  future of, 190–92
  negative reputation, xiii
  personal. *See* Personal ambitions
  (*See also* Raw ambition)
Ambition, rules
  balance, 113–38
  belief, 159–88
  belonging, 47–81
  discovery, 1–24
  focus, 25–45
  maturity, 139–58
  momentum, 83–111
Ambition addiction, avoiding
  cross-over planning, 122–24
  non-vocational responsibilities, 120–22
  realistic decision-making, 124–26
Ambitionist
  defined, xv–xvi, xviii, 50
  vs. dreamers, 23
Ambitious malaise, 174
Amnesty International, 178
Anger, 122 (*See also* Rage)
Anticipation, 84–85, 91, 92–93, 97–98, 101
Antinori, Piero, 137
Anxiety, 114, 119 (*See also* Connection anxiety)

Appreciation
  for customer, 69, 169
  for team member. *See* Peer recognition
Apprentice, 7, 16–17, 23
Arrogance, 37 (*See also* Self-aggrandizement)
Athletes, 90–93, 98, 100–1, 106–7, 147–48, 151–53
Audience, targeting, 62–63
Avoidance accountability, 78–79

Backup plans, 75
Balance, xvi, 113–16, 135–38
  threats to:
    addiction, 117–26
    alienation, 118, 126–30
    seclusion, 118, 131–35
Bailey, Chris, 43
Ballet, 123–24, 127, 134–35, 154, 181
Balsillie, Jim, 36–38, 42, 45
Bargaining chips, 93–94, 101
Barker, Cheryl, 120–21, 124
Baruch, Bernard M., 153
Belief, 159–60
  re-evaluating:
    alignments, 160, 162–67
    callings, 161, 169–73
    legacy, leaving, 161–62, 186–87
    reinventing yourself, 161, 173–83
    unpredictability, 161, 183–86
    values, updating, 161, 167–69
Bell Ontario, 142
Bella magazine, 184
Belonging, 47–50, 167
  strategies:
    following, assembling, 51, 59–69
    leadership style, deciding, 51, 70–73
    lifeboat team, choosing, 51, 54–59
    team, propelling, 51, 73–79
    tips, 79–81
    values, defining, 50, 52–54
Bend It like Beckham, 35
Benincasa, Robyn, 25–28, 39–40, 45
Berezhnaya, Elena, 151
Bergdorf Goodman, 105
Bergson, Henri, 154
Berkson, Eleanor Lambert, 80–81
Bernhard, Sandra, 96
Berry, John, 99
Best in Show, 52
Beverage industry, 140–41
Biotech industry, 10–11
Birch, Michael, 140–42, 144
BlackBerry, 36, 42, 119
Blair Witch Project, The, 99–100
Blass, Bill, 80
Board of directors, personal, 135
Bobos in Paradise (Brooks), 156–57, 191
Body, 163, 164, 165
Body language, 76
Bombardiers (Bronson), 116
Boredom, 29, 35–36, 102
Bounce-back, 143–58 (*See also* Serial bounce-back)
Boundaries, finding. *See* Comfort factor; Pain threshold
Brand, Claire, 53
Branding, 50, 51, 52–53, 60, 62, 67, 68, 80, 105–6, 141
Bravery. *See* Courage
Brinkley, Christie, 94
Bristol Old Vic Theatre School, 32
Broadway Cares, 103
Broadway Equity Fights AIDS, 103
Bronson, Po, 116–17, 121, 126, 127–28, 166
Brooks, David, 156–57, 191
Brown, Hilary, 85, 106, 125–26, 128, 130

Bruckheimer, Jerry, 5
Buddakan Restaurant, 95, 110
Bulldog: Spirit of the New Entrepreneur (Rubin), xi, xv, 50, 192

CAA (talent agency), 4
Callas, Marie, 120
Calling, 170–73
Calvin Klein (company), 169
Camaraderie, 65 (*See also* Belonging)
Camp, EJ, 83–85, 91, 93–94, 97–98, 107, 109
Canada, work/life conflicts, 113–14
Canadian Coalition on Acid Rain, 55, 56, 58
Canten, Dan, 60–63, 75
Canten, Dean, 60–63, 75
Caprion Pharmaceuticals Inc., 11
Career and Lifework Center (Univ. of Manitoba), xiii
Career Innovation Group, 167
Carleton University (Ottawa), 63
Carlotto, Franco, 176–77, 181, 187
Caron, Guy, 14
Carsen, Robert, 31–33, 40–41, 45
Catalysts, 63–66, 81
CBC, 58
CBC Montreal, 125
CBC Radio (Paris), 125
CBS, 5
Censorship, avoiding. *See* Self-censorship
Centers for Disease Control and Prevention, 114
Central School of Speech & Drama (London), 32
Champions, 55, 56, 57–58, 59 (*See also* Heroes; Mentors)
Chan Hon Goh, 123–24, 127, 134–35, 154, 181
Change
    attraction to, 98

    catalysts for, 63–66
    resistance to, 22
    (*See also* Discovery)
Character building, 143, 153–54
    choice, 155
    fear, 154
    performance, 156–57
    power, 155–56
    responsibility, 155
Cheeky Chops, 180
Children, 120, 121, 130, 132–33, 190
Choice, 155, 192 (*See also* Decision-making)
Choreography, 88–90, 103–4, 110–11, 181
Circus Roncalli, 14
Cirque du Soleil, 12–15
CITES (Convention on International Trade in Endangered Species), 150–51, 155
Citytv, 54
Clarkson, Adrienne, 58
Collaborations, 103–4
Collins, Jim, 163, 168
Color of Money, The, 94
Columbia Pictures, 4
Comfort factor, 65–66
Commitment, 51, 54, 57, 76–77, 80, 118, 129, 161, 167
Competition, 87, 104–6
Complacency, 109
Compromises, 40
Conference Board of Canada, 114
Confessors. *See* Mentors
Confidence, 15, 16, 18, 21–22, 83
Conflict
    and alienation avoidance, 129
    and back-up plans, 75
    fear of, 74–76
    head/heart, 164–67
    and leadership style, 70, 71
    minimizing, 51

and personal ambitions, 75
values, 191
(*See also* Work/life balance)
Connection anxiety, 119, 127
Consensus, 148
Consulting profession, 105
Consumer loyalty. *See* Branding
Contact, 22
Continental Restaurant, 95, 109
Contingency plans, 75
Continual learning, 44–45
Control, loss of, 20, 40
Conversations, peer-to-peer. *See* Myth making; Storytelling
Core communities, creating. *See* Belonging
Costume Institute (NYC), 80
Cott Beverages, 141
Coty Awards, 80
Council of Fashion Designers of America, 80
Courage, 19–20, 31–33, 45, 166
Creativity, 8, 10, 14, 18, 66
Cross-media storytelling, 99–100
Cross-over planning, 117, 120, 124, 133, 135
Cruise, Tom, 94, 97–98, 156
CSI (TV show), 1, 5
CSI Miami (TV show), 5–6
Curiosity, 102, 149–51
Curve, staying ahead of, 104–6
Cushing, Robert, 108
Customer, respect for, 69, 169

Dance. *See* Ballet; Choreography
Davis, Melinda, 114, 115, 132
de Bono, Edward, 18
de la Renta, Oscar, 80–81
De Vlaamse Opera, 120
Dean Witter, 2
Decision-making
focused, 28–30
head vs. heart, 164–67
strategies:
emotional elements, minimizing, 33–36
insight, 40–42
optimistic opportunists, 42–44
pain threshold, 29, 30–33
timing, 36–40
Dedication, 17, 42 (*See also* Calling; Commitment)
Depression, 114, 115
Designers, 60–66, 67–69, 77, 104, 105
(*See also* Fashion industry; Industrial design; Interior design)
Designers Guild (UK), 65–66, 68
Desires, 7, 8–9, 162
Desjardins, Clarissa, 10–11, 23
Detachment, 71, 76, 106–8, 126, 136, 147
Detail, attention to, 51, 78–79, 96–97, 98, 101
Determination, 20, 27, 83, 95
Deutsche Opera Berlin, 120
Diana, Princess of Wales, 184
Diesel, 169
Disability pensions, 115
Discovery
defined, 6
dreamers vs. ambitionists, 23
strategies:
apprenticing, 7, 16–17
desires, facing, 7, 8–9
and intuition, 8, 20–22
questions, asking, 7, 9–12
and self-censorship, 8, 17–20
spontaneity, 7, 12–16
and trial and error, 22
(*See also* Rediscovery)
Disney, Walt, 144
Diversification, 133–34
Douglas Hospital Research Centre (Montreal), 10
Dreamers, 22, 28
vs. ambitionists, 23

Driven to Excel: A Portrait of Canada's Workaholics (Kemeny), xiv
Dry Spell, A (Maloney), 156
D-Squared, 60–63, 75
Dysfunction (team), profiles, 73–79

Early retirement, 115
East of Eden (Steinbeck), 192
Eco Challenge (Fiji), 25, 39–40
Edison, Thomas A., 143
Editor role, 88, 102–4, 168
Elitism, 128, 191 (*See also* Arrogance; Self-aggrandizement; Status)
Ellis, Havelock, 139
Emotion Marketing (Robinette/Brand), 53
Emotionalism, 35, 37, 71, 162 (*See also* Head/heart conflict)
Employee
 retention, 49
 termination, 76, 165–66
Endorsements, athletic, 100–1
Energy, monitoring/focusing. *See* Momentum, sustaining
Engagement, rules of, 128–29
English National Opera, 120
Enlightened self-interest, 62
Enron, xiii
Entrepreneur
 defined, xv, 50
 mystique of, 52
 (*See also* Magician, leadership style)
Environmental issues, 55–59, 62, 63, 149–51, 155
Etiquette, 69, 128, 169
Etiquette (Post), 69
European Union, mental health, 115
Exclusivity, 128 (*See also* Elitism; Status)
Exploitation, 117
Exploration, 7, 9, 19–20, 24
Expo 67 (Montreal), 63
Eye contact, 76

Failure
 bounce-back:
  curiosity, fostering, 149–51
  rejection, embracing, 143, 144–45
  serial bounce-back, 144, 151–53
  skills assessment, 143, 145–48
  and strength of character, 144, 153–57
 learning from, xvi, 139–43
Faith, 177
Fame, 8, 174
Family/work life, balance. *See* Work/life balance
Fashion Cares/AIDS Awareness, 178
Fashion industry, 54, 60–63, 67–68, 69, 75, 80–81, 93–94, 164–65, 166–67, 168–69, 183–84
Fashion Oscare de la Mode, 60
Fashion Television, 54
Fassett, Kaffe, 68
Fast Company, 98–99, 101, 136
Faulkner, Bob, 147–48, 154, 158
Fear
 admitting to, 154
 of conflict, 74–76
 factor, 66 (*See also* Comfort factor)
 of humiliation, 76
Federation of Canadian Naturalists, 56
Festival mondial du cirque de demain, 14
Fifteen (restaurant), 180–81
Film industry, 4–5, 33–36, 43–44, 77, 99, 105
Final results mode, 4, 23
Finance industry, 77
Finland, stress-related illness, 114
First Nations, 141–42
First Nations Buying Group, 142
First Nations Cola, 141
First $20 Million's Always the Hardest, The (Bronson), 116
Fitness for Kids, 176–77
Five Dysfunctions of a Team, The (Lencioni), 73

Focus, 25–45 (*See also* Decision-making)
Following, creating, 59–60, 166, 167
  change catalysts, 63–66
  participation factor, 60–63
  pluralism, appeal of, 66–68
  pride of ownership, 68–69
Ford, Henry, 145
Fossett, Steve, 144–45
Four Seasons Hotel (Tokyo), 86
Four Seasons Hotels and Resorts, 105
Franks, Lynne, 177–80, 182–83
Franks, Simon, 33–36, 37–38, 43–44, 45
Free fall, 7, 15–16 (*See also* Spontaneity)
Freedom, 135–36
Friendships, workplace, 128
Fritz, Robert, 146, 147
Frustration, 38
Full Monty, The, 88, 103
Fuller, Buckminster, 63

Gall, Hughes, 41–42
Gandhi, Mohandas, 176
Garbo Trashcan, 67
Generalists, 67 (*See also* Pluralists; Specialists)
Germany, stress-related illness, 114
Gerry Cottle Circus School, 13
Getty, John Paul, 113
Gibbons, Yulles, 95
Girls Intelligence Agency, 190
Gladwell, Malcolm, 99
Globe and Mail, 113
Good Morning America, 184
Good to Great (Collins), 163, 168
G-Push, 100–1
Graciousness, 169
Grand & Toy, 142
Greenpeace, 178
Guild, Tricia, 65–66, 68, 69, 78–79, 104
Gypsy Rose, 88, 111

Hairspray, 88
Hallmark, 53
Hamnett, Katharine, 178
Handheld computing, 36
Happiness quotient, 166–67, 190
Harlem Globetrotters, 4
Hawaii Ironman Race (2002), 100
Head/heart/body/soul, aligning, 160, 162–67
Head/heart conflict, 164–67
Heindorff, Michael, 68
Helmsley Building (NYC), 84
Hepburn, Katharine, 169
Heroes, 77, 176, 177
Hiatus, reigniting momentum, 108–10
High-tech industry, 36–38, 52, 116–17
Hodgkin, Howard, 68
Holyfield, Evander, 92
Honesty, 74 (*See also* Self-knowledge)
Humiliation, fear of, 76
Humour, 76, 95
Hurley, Adèle, 55–59, 62, 63
Hush Puppy shoes, 99
Hyatt International, 105

Iams (pet food), 62
ideaCity conference, 54–55
Identity, sense of, 52, 53 (*See also* Belonging; Branding)
Illness, stress-related, 114–15
Imagination. *See* Creativity
Imparato, Silvia, 137
In and Out, 88
In Concert, 95
Independence, 49, 77–78
Individuality, xviii, 66
Industrial design, 63–64, 68–69, 104
Influencers, political arena, 55–56 (*See also* Leadership profiles)
Information, analyzing, 29, 35, 37, 38
Insight, acting on, 30, 40–42
Inspiration, xiv, 65, 109, 147, 175–80, 191

"Inspiration and Work" survey, 167
Interior design, 65–66, 68, 86–87, 102, 105–6
International Best Dressed Poll, 80–81
International Labour Organization, 114, 115
Intuition, 8, 14, 20–22, 23, 32–33, 35, 71, 162, 166, 184–85
Iron Man contest, 100, 147–48

Jack Spade (company), 183–84
Jackson, Charles, 167
Johnson, Samuel, 149
Jokes, 76
Jones, Roy, Jr., 90, 92

Keller, Ed, 99
Kelly, Grace, 169
Kemeny, Anna, xiv
King/queen, leadership style, 71, 75, 76, 81
King, Warrior, Magician, Lover (Moore), 70

La Scala Milan, 33
LAMDA (London), 32
Laporte, Barbara, xiii
Larry King Live, 174
Lateral thinking, 10, 71
Laughter, 76 (*See also* Humor)
Leadership profiles, 51, 70
  king/queen, 71, 75, 76, 81
  lover, 71, 77–78, 81
  magician, 71–72, 73, 81
  warrior, 70–71, 77, 81
Leadership style
  assessing, 72–73
  and barriers to teamwork, 74, 75, 76, 77, 78, 79
Learning
  continual, 18, 44–45
  discovery stage, 7
  from mistakes, xvi, 45, 139–43

and open-mindedness, 6
from setbacks, 127, 131
Legacy, 186–87
Lencioni, Patrick, 51, 73
Leverage, defined, 93
Leveragers, lifeboat team, 55, 58–59
Leveraging
  marketing tools, 101
  talent/skills, 93–94, 101
Liceu (Barcelona), 33
Lieberman, Susan S., 149–51, 155
Life balance. *See* Work/life balance
Lifeboat team, 51, 54–57
  champions, 55, 56, 57–58, 59
  leveragers, 55, 58–59, 80–81
  momentum builders, 58, 59
Lillehammer Olympics (1994), 152
Limitations, self-imposed. *See* Self-censorship
Limits, setting, 122–26
Listening, 74, 128, 134
Lobbyists, 55–59, 75, 77
London Fashion Week, 178
Loneliness, 126 (*See also* Alienation; Seclusion)

Madonna, 60, 96
Magician, leadership style, 71–72, 74, 81
Maloney, Susan, 156
Management by objectives (MBOs), 148
Manitoba Telecom Services, 142
Manners, 69, 128
Marketing
  athletic endorsements, 100–1
  on internet, 99–100
Martin, Ricky, 60
Materialism, 8, 191
Maturity, 139–58 (*See also* Failure, bounce-back)
Maximum Energy for Life (Shilstone), 90
McCormack, Chris, 100–1

McGill University, 10
McGillis, Kelly, 97–98
Media coverage, 55, 57, 58
Medical profession, 70–73, 186–87, 188
Mediocrity, 102
Memorial Sloan-Kettering Cancer Center (NYC), 170
Mendes, Sam, 110–11
Mental illness, 114–16
Mentors, xviii, 57–58, 134–35, 180–81
Mephistopheles (opera), 41–42
Merrill Lynch, 2, 10
Metropolitan Museum of Art (NYC), 80
Metropolitan Opera, 33
MGM, 105
Mirage Hotel (Las Vegas), 2, 4, 10
Mistakes, learning from, xvi, 45, 139–43 (*See also* Failure, bounce-back)
Mitchell, Jerry, 88–90, 103–4, 110–11, 181
Mizrahi, Isaac, 99
Models, 75, 93–94 (*See also* Fashion industry)
Modern Women's Handbook (Franks), 179
Momentum
  barriers to, 84
  builders, 55, 58, 59, 80–81
  defined, 85, 86–87
  strategies:
    developing, 87, 88–102
    reigniting, 88, 108–10
    sustaining, 102–8
Momentum, developing
  leveraging talent, 93–94
  performance management, 90–93
  readiness, 88–90
  storytelling and myth making, 98–101
  what you do best, 98
  working your trade, 94–98
Momentum, managing, 83–85
Momentum, reigniting, 108
  building on outtakes, 109
  creating traction, 109–10
Momentum, sustaining
  counteracting competition, 104–6
  editor role, 102–4, 168
  performance management, 106–8
Montevetrano Wines, 137
Moore, Roger, 70
Morimoto (restaurant), 67, 95
Mother Teresa, 176
Motivation, xiv, 16, 27, 65, 80, 121
MuchMusic, 54
Muhammad Ali, 176
Museum of Modern Art (NYC), 63
Music Man, The, 89
Myth making, 98–101

Nambé, 64, 67
National Alliance of Breast Cancer Organizations, 170
National Ballet of Canada, 123
National Cancer Institute, 170
National Post, xi
NBC, 95
NBC News, 125
Negotiations, 108–9
Networking, 19, 21
New Culture of Desire, The (Davis), 114, 132
New York Stock Exchange, 119
Newman, Paul, 180
Newman, Scott, 180
Newman's Own (foods), 180
Next Group (US), 115
Nike, 52
Norton, Larry, 170–73, 186–87, 188
Nudist on the Late Shift, The (Bronson), 116

Obst, Linda, 22
Ochsner Clinic Foundation, 90
Oh Chair, 67

Oliver, Jamie, 180–81
Olympics, 151, 152, 153
Open-mindedness, 6, 9, 15, 19–20, 120
Opéra de Genève, 41–42
Opponents, identifying, 91–92, 101
Opportunities
  assessing, 87
  benchmarking, 20
Optimists, 30, 42–44, 72
Outtakes, 109
Overeagerness, 108
Ownership, sense of. *See* Belonging

Pacing yourself, 39–40, 84–85, 87, 104, 106, 107, 145 (*See also* Momentum)
Paging architectures, 36–37
Pain
  physical, 114
  threshold, 29, 30–33, 42
Palm Pilot, 36
Paralysis. *See* Self-censorship
Parenting, 120, 121, 130, 190 (*See also* Work/life balance)
Paris Opera, 33, 42
Parker, Robert, 137–38
Parsons School of Design, 60
Participation, 51, 60–63, 81, 128–29
Partnership, 52
Passion, 23, 88, 116–17, 123, 126, 137, 147, 149, 177
Path of Least Resistance, The (Fritz), 146
Patience, 38–39, 181
Paw Paw Village Players, 89
Peer recognition, 55, 75, 125
Pensions, disability, 115
Pepsi Co., 84
Performance
  aspect, maturity, 156–57
  management, 90–93, 106–8
Performing arts, 88–90, 103–4, 110–11, 120–21, 123–24, 127, 134–35, 154
Personal ambitions, 75, 76, 79, 91

Personal board, 135
Personal digital assistants, 36
Personal values
  redefining, xvi
  vs. vocational demands, xiv
  (*See also* Values)
Personal worth, 49
Personality, addictive, 117
Perspective
  long-term, 18, 119
  maintaining, 18, 146
Philanthropy. *See* Altruism
Photographers, 83–85, 93–94, 97–98, 107, 109
Pluralists, 66–68, 81 (*See also* Generalists; Specialists)
Poland, stress-related illness, 114
Politeness, 69, 128, 169
Pollution Probe, 56
Polygram, 43
Possibilties, focus on, 30, 42–44, 192
Post-career life. *See* Cross-over planning
Power, 8, 55, 74, 125, 143, 155–56
Pragmatism, 94, 129, 144–48, 183
Pratt Institute (NYC), 63
Preparedness, 88–90, 92–93, 96–98
Pride, 68–69, 80, 81, 92
Principal Dance Supplies, 124
Prioritizing, importance of, 38–39
Prix de Lausanne (Switzerland), 123
Professionalism, 17, 34, 182
Pushelberg, Glenn, 86, 102, 105–6

Queen, leadership style. *See* King/queen, leadership style
Questions, asking, 7, 9–12

Rage, 114
Raid Gauloises, 25–27
Rashid, Karim, 63–64, 68–69, 104
Raw ambition, xv, 10, 50, 177, 187, 191
Reagan administration, 56

Rebounding. *See* Bounce-back
Redbus, 33–35
Rediscovery, 4, 6, 7
Reflection, 127–28, 144, 145–48, 157–58, 175 (*See also* Self-knowledge)
Reinventing yourself, 161, 173–85
Rejection, embracing, 18–19, 143, 144–45, 146–47
Research In Motion (RIM), 36–38, 42
Respect, 69, 169
Respectability, 143, 149, 150, 151, 155
Responsiblity, 155
Restaurant Hospitality, 95
Restaurateurs, 95–97, 107, 109–10, 181–82
Results, inattention to, 78–79
Rhode Island School of Design, 63, 64
Risk
   aversion to, 98
   incorporating, 7, 15, 22, 67
   and warrior, 70–71
Robinette, Scott, 53
Rochester Institute of Technology, 93
Rocky Horror Show, The, 88, 103
Rogers, Rita, 185–85
Rolling Stone, 83, 94
Roper ASW, 99
Rubin, Harriet, 8–9
Ruiz, John, 92
Rumors, 99
Rundgren, Todd, 95
Runner, The (screenplay), 3–4

Sacrifices, 29, 30, 118, 120, 121, 129–31
St. Louis Cardinals, 90
Salzberg Festival, 33
Saviors. *See* Mentors
Scandals, xiii
Scent of a Woman, 88
Schoultz, Basil, 13, 14
Scott, Wayne, 131–32, 146, 154

Scott Newman Foundation, 180
Seclusion, avoiding
   diversification, 133–35
   saviors/confessors, 134–35
   and time management, 131–33
Second discipline, 83, 85–86
Security, xiii, 22, 84
SEED, 179
Seed Handbook, The (Franks), 179
Seinfeld, Jerry, 96
Self-aggrandizement, 119, 126, 128, 131
Self-censorship, 6, 8, 17–20, 23
Self-directed progress, 87
Self-esteem, 18, 49
Self-fulfillment, 149–51, 166, 180, 190
Self-help books, 115, 132
Self-knowledge, 73–74, 37, 90–91, 93, 113, 125, 157–58, 175 (*See also* Reflection)
Self-preservation, 115
September 11, 2001, xiii, xiv, 38, 84–85, 109
Serendipity, 7, 122, 183, 184 (*See also* Spontaneity)
Serial bounce-back, 144, 151–53
Setbacks, learning from. *See* Bounce-back
Shared destiny, 78
Shilstone, Michael, 90–93, 96, 98, 106–7, 168
Side time, 132–33
Sikharulidze, Anton, 152–53
Silicon Valley, 116
Six Degrees of Separation, 122
Six Thinking Hats (de Bono), 18
Skills
   assessing, 143, 145–48, 157
   collectors, 132
   leveraging, 93–94, 101
Sleep disorders, 114
Sleepless in Seattle, 22
Sliakhov, Oleg, 152

Smith, Adam, 62
Smith, Ozzie, 90, 98
Social exclusion. *See* Alienation, avoiding
Soul, 163, 164, 165, 191
Spade, Andy, 164–65, 166–67, 168–69, 183–84
Spade, Kate, 19–20, 67–68, 69, 164–65, 166, 168–69
Specialists, 66, 67 (*See also* Generalists; Pluralists)
Spinks, Michael, 90
Spontaneity, 7, 12–16, 23
and setting limits, 122–26
Sports enhancement industry, 100–1
Starbucks, 52
Starr, Stephen, 95–97, 107, 109–10
Stars on Ice, 151
Starwood Hotels & Resorts, 105
Status, 8, 36, 135, 143, 191
Steinbeck, John, 192
Stock market, xiii, 38, 52, 109 (*See also* Trader mentality)
Storytelling, 98–101
Strengths, assessing, 145–48, 157, 182 (*See also* Reflection; Self-knowledge)
Stress-related illness, 114–16
Success, intoxication of, 118–19
Sui, Anna, 99
Superiority, sense of, 37, 118–19 (*See also* Elitism; Self-aggrandizement)
Support team. *See* Lifeboat team

Talents. *See* Skills
Tassler, Nina, 5
Tchalenko, Janice, 68
Team dysfunctions
absence of trust, 73–74
avoidance accountability, 77–78
fear of conflict, 74–76
inattention to results, 78–79
lack of commitment, 76–77
and leadership style, 74, 75, 76, 77, 78, 79

Television production, 5, 105, 125
Terrorism, xiii (*See also* September 11, 2001)
Textile design, 65–66, 68, 104
Therapy Dogs International, 121
Tiffany & Co. (NYC), 105
Time magazine, 151
Time management, 131–33
Timing, 29–30, 36–40, 122, 124, 162
Tipping Point, The (Gladwell), 99
Top Gun, 94, 97–98
Toronto Star, 56
Tosca, 120
Tourism industry, 62, 63
Toxic relationships, 134–35
Toys R Us, 142
Track record, 100–1
Traction, creating, 109–10
Trader mentality, 34–36
Travel & Leisure magazine, 95
Trend tracking, 109
Trial and error, 22, 29–30
Trust, 8, 23, 51, 73–74, 78

Umbra, 67
UN Beijing Women's Conference (1995), 179
United States, stress-related illness, 114, 115
Universal Studios, 43
University of Arts (Philadelphia), 63
University of Minnesota, xiii
Unknown
embracing, 16, 20
fear of, 7
(*See also* Unpredictability)
Unpredictability, 161, 183–86 (*See also* Unknown)
Upside, calculating, 35, 37–38, 39–40
U2, 96

Validation, 18, 19
external, 23, 149, 150, 151, 187, 188

Values
  defining, 50, 52–54
  questioning, xiii
  updating, 161, 167–69
Vancouver Opera, 120
Vanity, 29
Vanity Fair, 144
Viacom, 95
Vienna State Opera, 33
Volunteer work, 103–4, 117, 121, 122
  (*See also* Altruism)

W hotels (NYC), 86, 105
Warrior, leadership style, 70–71, 77, 81
Watson, Albert, 93
Watson, Andrew, 12–15, 22, 23
Weaknesses, assessing, 145–48, 157 (*See also* Reflection; Self-knowledge)
Webber, Bruce, 93
West Side Story, 89
What Should I Do with My Life? (Bronson), 116
Whyte, Ken, xi–xii
Will Rogers Follies, 103
William Morris Agency, 3
Wine industry, 137–38
Winners-and-losers attitude, 71
Wolverine, 99
Woodward, Joanne, 180

Word of mouth. *See* Myth making; Storytelling
Work/life balance, xiii, xiv, 6, 114–16, 120–22, 129, 132, 133, 136, 138, 175
Workaholism, xiii–xiv, 113–14, 127
Working your trade, 87, 94–98, 101, 103
Workplace-induced stress, 114–16
World Boxing Association (WBA), 92
World Figure Skating Championships, 152, 153
World Trade Center, 84–85 (*See also* September 11, 2001)
World Wildlife Fund International, 149, 150–51
Wurman, Richard Saul, 54

Xerox, 142

Yabu, George, 86–87, 102
Yabu Pushelberg, 86–87, 102–3, 104, 105
York University (Toronto), 31–32
Young Americans (dance troupe), 89

Znaimer, Moses, 54
Zuiker, Anthony E., 1–6, 7, 10, 11, 18, 22, 23

CPSIA information can be obtained
at www.ICGtesting.com
Printed in the USA
LVHW04s1851101018
593100LV00002B/727/P